LEADING
COHERENTLY
Reflections From Leaders
Around the World

Nancy Stanford-Blair
Cardinal Stritch University
Michael H. Dickmann
Cardinal Stritch University

SAGE Publications
Thousand Oaks ▪ London ▪ New Delhi

For information:

Sage Publications, Inc.
2455 Teller Road
Thousand Oaks, California 91320
E-mail: order@sagepub.com

Sage Publications Ltd.
1 Oliver's Yard
55 City Road
London EC1Y 1SP
United Kingdom

Sage Publications India Pvt. Ltd.
B-42, Panchsheel Enclave
Post Box 4109
New Delhi 110 017 India

Library of Congress Cataloging-in-Publication Data

Stanford-Blair, Nancy.
Leading coherently: Reflections from leaders around the world / Nancy Stanford-Blair and Michael H. Dickmann.
    p. cm.
Includes bibliographical references and index.
ISBN 1-4129-0589-3 (pbk.)
   1. Leadership. 2. Executive ability. 3. Employee motivation. I. Dickmann, Michael Haley. II. Title.
HD57.7.S717 2005
658.4'092—dc22   2004023044

This book is printed on acid-free paper.

05 06 07 08 10 9 8 7 6 5 4 3 2 1

Acquisitions Editor:	Al Bruckner
Editorial Assistant:	MaryAnn Vail
Production Editor:	Denise Santoyo
Typesetter:	C&M Digitals (P) Ltd.
Indexer:	Kathy Paparchontis
Cover Designer:	Michelle Lee Kenny

LEADING
COHERENTLY

*Dedicated to thirty-six coherent leaders
with gratitude
for their wisdom and generosity*

Contents

Prologue

The Quest

Each and every leader, whether the CEO of a multinational corporation or a school principal, can become more effective—much more effective—by focusing on a small number of core aspects of leadership and by developing a new mind-set about the leader's responsibility to himself or herself and to those with whom he or she works.

—Fullan (2001, p. 2)

What is leadership? Are definable attributes apparent when done well? What sustains leadership and those who engage in it? Does it differ in practice by context, content, or culture? As any student of leadership knows, answers to such questions remain elusive. Leadership has intrigued humanity over the millennia. Yet, as a formal field of study, it is relatively young, and although theories and formulas abound, conclusive understanding of the phenomenon is less accessible (Antonakis, Cianciolo, & Sternberg, 2004). The quest for deeper understanding nevertheless continues at the beginning of this new century. It is a quest fueled by concern as the quality of local, national, and international leadership is increasingly called into question.

On awakening to the serious problems our planet faces, from balancing budgets to the consequences of global warming, we find ourselves pressed to find leaders who can be relied on to serve our organization, locale, country, and planet. Wheatley (2002) has observed that we are in a time of increasing economic and political instability, growing divisiveness, and fear of failing systems. With the sense that we have painted ourselves into some very serious corners comes the awareness that leadership is in demand. Fullan (2001) captured this sentiment in observing that the requisite "effective leadership is in very short supply" (p. xii). Indeed, at a time when our need is greatest, many perceive that the supply of quality leaders has peaked or perhaps diminished (Connet & Carmera, 2001; Ferrandino & Tirozzi, 2000). It is a shortage that confronts a board of directors searching for a CEO, a nation seeking to elect a prime minister or president, or a school system hunting for a new principal or superintendent. Good leaders, it would appear, are increasingly hard to come by. Such perceptions of a leadership shortage might merely reflect the anxiety endured by every generation when facing their own particular challenges. It is a perception, nonetheless, that encourages the pursuit of further knowledge about the nature and nurture of leadership.

Participants in this ongoing quest for better understanding of the phenomenon quickly come to the understanding that leadership is complex and contextual. For that reason, it is a concept that is often deconstructed and examined in parts and from different perspectives in the interest of gaining greater understanding of the whole. In this vein, our recent efforts— *Connecting Leadership to the Brain* (Dickmann & Stanford-Blair, 2002) and *Leading With the Brain in Mind* (Dickmann, Stanford-Blair, & Rosati-Bojar, 2004)—focused on the nature of human capacity and how leaders might best influence such capacity toward the achievement of goals. Our focus this time was on leadership formation, performance, and sustainability. Our interest was in examining how leaders are formed to the task of influencing the capacity of others, how they perform such influence, and how they sustain their influence over time.

To that end, this project engaged 36 exemplary leaders in reflective conversation about their work. Specifically, it employed an interview protocol to structure reflection about (a) how leaders are formed, (b) how leaders perform to influence others, and (c) how leaders sustain themselves and their leadership influence. The participating leaders were purposefully selected to represent diversity in culture, gender, and experience. Thirty-six interviews, 34 planes, 5 continents, and 36,000 miles later, the leaders' stories generated a wealth of knowledge and insight. The challenging task of analyzing over 1,000 pages of transcripts and field notes followed.

While it is not possible or profitable to relate the entire narrative shared in the interviews, what you will find within the following pages are valuable insights and prominent themes about how leadership was formed, performed, and sustained by 36 leaders. You will also observe how a coherent relationship between formation, performance, and sustainability expands the consequence of leadership.

Whatever your current leadership status, we hope you will fully participate in the reflective conversations that follow—and thereby further advance your quest for leadership knowledge and effectiveness.

NSB & MHD

Acknowledgments

With an undertaking of this magnitude, many people were enlisted for support, guidance, and technical assistance. Insightful nominations and subsequent connections to exemplary leaders produced a rich and varied pool of participants. Moving from East to West, our gratitude is extended to Tom Runyan, Jeanette Mitchell, Mary Kellner, Mike Peoples, and Jill Heuer in the United States. For Asian and South Pacific contacts, we appreciated the assistance provided by Gary Rasmussen, Paul Blair, Rod Chamberlain, Angela Rosati, Kevin O'Carroll, and Ross Gilbert. In Eastern and Western Europe, Nancy and Tom Tiernan, CJ Nickerson, and Andy Hargraves provided both connections and logistical support. Finally, in Africa, Peter and Dinah Annor offered guidance and friendship. Further appreciation is extended to those listed above who went beyond the call to offer their homes and friendship to the researchers.

Alexis Blair, Ron Lange, and Pat Magestro assisted the interview process, and their detailed field notes and insights about emerging themes were invaluable.

Post-interview technical assistance came from several quarters. Angela McCormick Blair contributed countless hours to the transcription of interview tapes. Mike Ashcraft formatted audio and video clips. Nicholas Blair lent his creativity to conceptualizing the visual models used in the text.

As always, the support of family was essential to the completion of this project, including the extended family of supportive colleagues at Cardinal Stritch University. The enthusiastic support of Al Bruckner at Sage Publications was an added bonus.

Introduction

Talking Leadership

I believe that we can change the world if we start listening to each other again. Simple, honest, human conversation. Not meditation, negotiation, problem-solving, debate, or public meetings. Simple, truthful conversation where we have a chance to speak, we each feel heard, and we each listen well.

—Wheatley (2002, p. 3)

Talking Story

Ideas, values, and lessons have long been communicated through story. Shared for millions of years in communal gatherings over evening fires, stories communicate important information from generation to generation during times of celebration, challenge, and change. Whether shared in the oral tradition, painted on cave walls, carved in stone, printed on paper, or portrayed through song or film, stories consolidate the human experience. Thus, it is in the tradition of story that powerful lessons drawn from contemporary leaders will be passed along to you in this book.

Reflect for a moment about occasions when you have experienced meaningful conversations with friends and colleagues about the work you do—what you do and how you do it and why you keep doing it even when the chips are down. In sharing your challenges, successes, and failures with another, it is likely that you realized some new insight from the exchange. In Hawaiian tradition, such discourse is known as "talking story," a conversation in which you share something about yourself with others. It is said in that tradition that by talking story, the degrees of separation between people melt away, creating new understandings across cultures and contexts. This book tapped the power of that ancient practice to collect and report the reflections of a unique group of leaders from around the world as they "talked story" about their leadership. The product is a collective story that passes on their insights about how they came to leadership, how they lead, and how they sustain their leadership efforts. More important, the process used to capture the reflective wisdom of exemplary leaders provides a framework by which all leaders can productively "talk leadership"—a framework that engages the power of reflective conversation within self and with others to gain insight about how effective leadership is formed, performed, and sustained.

Storytellers

The storytellers who contribute to the leadership conversations that follow in this book are 36 exemplars of contemporary leadership practice across diverse contexts throughout the world, plus one additional source. That additional rich source of leadership lore is you, the reader.

THIRTY-SIX EXEMPLARS

If you wanted to identify exemplary leaders who were worthy of a conversation about leadership, how would you find them? Identify the current favorites of business and politics? Look in *Who's Who?* Conduct a scientific survey? Consult the leading authorities on leadership? While all of those methods hold promise, they each have shortcomings. The current favorites of business and politics might be in disfavor (if not in jail or out of office) tomorrow, and those presented in *Who's Who* are often self-nominated or have paid for such print recognition. A survey assumes a base of widely accepted criteria for effective leadership, and the recommendations of leading authorities would most likely be filtered through their own espoused theories of leadership.

> If John Hood goes, I go. . . . He's that good.
>
> —*John Graham, Chancellor of Auckland University*

A more straightforward method for identifying exemplary leaders was used in this investigation, one partially based on the intuitive human sense of "knowing good leadership when we see it." We all, of course, have our individual biases about what good leadership is, based on our personal knowledge and experience. Yet, most would agree that when we find a leader who communicates a clear and compelling purpose and who positively engages and supports people in the process of successfully achieving that purpose, we are inclined to celebrate.

With faith in others' ability to recognize effective leadership when they encounter it, credible contacts (i.e., individuals who had backgrounds in the formal study of leadership and/or were acknowledged leaders in their own right) from around the world were asked to nominate candidates for participation in this study. To increase the likelihood that nominated leaders would be worth the interview, the following criteria were applied to the nomination process:

1. Nominees were to be individuals who fulfilled a basic definition of leadership as a process of influencing others toward the achievement of a goal (Dickmann & Stanford-Blair, 2002).

2. Nominees were to be leaders who were widely respected in their field, office, organization, or country—respected by both external and internal observers of their leadership.

3. Nominees were to be leaders who were known for successful results and goal achievements.

Taken independently, each criterion was important. Nominated candidates were either currently or recently involved in influential relationships with others for the purpose of achieving specific goals. Respect garnered from both within and outside of their leadership context brought forward candidates who were acknowledged by distant observers, as well as those who directly experienced their leadership (i.e., although reputations can be built on the outside of an organization, the "proof in the pudding" is often the ability to earn respect within the organization as well). This is important, as studies have found that organizations in which members rate their leaders positively are more productive and more financially viable (Denison, 1997; Zipkin, 2000). In addition, all of the nominated leaders had demonstrated that they could accomplish results, close the deal, realize goals, or otherwise fulfill a purpose. Research has frequently defined leadership success based on outcomes achieved and accounted for by tangible results, as well as reputation garnered (Day, 2001). It was not that the nominated leaders were not vulnerable to criticism and human failing. All leaders suffer that reality. Rather, the point is that they had earned leadership credibility.

The purposeful selection of a credible pool of exemplary leaders was further influenced by an interest in discovering universal leadership perspectives and practices across diverse contexts. The Global Leadership and Organizational Behavior Effectiveness (GLOBE) Project assesses the similarities and differences in the cultural semantic definition of leadership in 60 participating countries. Similar to the definition employed in this study, GLOBE researchers have defined leadership as the ability of an individual to influence, motivate, and enable others to contribute toward the effectiveness and success of the organization of which they are members (Den Hartog et al., 1999). Because comparative leadership research is somewhat uncommon, it was the intention of this investigation to advance the understanding of leadership across diverse contexts. Accordingly, 36 storytellers were purposefully selected to represent a diverse population of leaders. The intent was to portray leadership across its many and diverse manifestations—from the leadership represented by prominent politicians and corporate executives to representatives of the preponderance of leadership influence exerted more quietly and subtly in everyday relationships (Burns, 1978). As a result, nominated leaders were screened toward the selection of a rich cross-section of individuals who represented diversity in

- Context and experience
- Knowledge and expertise
- Roles and stations
- Culture and gender

Thanks to the generous efforts of many colleagues throughout the world, over 100 candidates were nominated as promising participants in this project. Subsequently, that nominated population was further screened, and contacts were made to solicit a core of 36 leaders who agreed to share their leadership stories. The talented, articulate, and diverse group of storytellers that emerged from the selection process included leaders in government, law, business, education, health, recreation, professional associations, and the arts. Figure 1 presents the 36 storytellers with descriptions of their leadership context by geographical location and positions and roles at the time they shared their stories. The stories shared by the 36 leaders emerge and mix in the chapters that follow and directly solicit your leadership story in the process.

PLUS ONE

The 36 interviewed leaders—a group diverse in culture, gender, roles, and spheres of influence—provided a deep well of experience and insight to draw on. That experience and insight will be progressively visited in succeeding chapters. As rich as such revelations might be, however, the purpose of *Leading Coherently* is not limited to discerning universal lessons from an accomplished group of leaders. An additional agenda arises from Wheatley's (2002) call for simple, honest conversation as quoted at the beginning of this introduction. That is, the intent of this book is to structure a leadership conversation that moves beyond the wisdom of 36 exemplars to encompass your leadership experience and that of other readers. To that end, you will be both invited and facilitated as an additional storyteller and active participant in *Leading Coherently*. It is an invitation to a conversation organized around four story lines.

Story Lines

The primary motivation for this work was to discover how individuals who were reputed exemplars of effective leadership came to be leaders, conducted themselves as leaders, and sustained themselves as leaders. Within this

Name	Location	Position and Role
Alex Banful	Accra, Ghana	Managing Director, GSMF International, an organization whose mission is the improvement of public health
Michael Barber	Great Britain, UK	Director, Prime Minister's Delivery Unit in charge of the implementation of Great Britain's Policy Reform
Richard Bissen	Hawaii	First Deputy Attorney General for the state of Hawaii
Chet Bradley	Wisconsin	Retired State Supervisor for Health Education in the state of Wisconsin
Tim Brighouse	Birmingham, UK	CEO of Birmingham Schools, the second largest school system in England
Rod Chamberlain	Hawaii	Headmaster, Kamehameha School, a private school for Hawaiian students
Boon Yoon Chiang	Singapore	CEO, Jardine-Matheson, Singapore Division of the largest trading company in Southeast Asia
PM Helen Clark	New Zealand	Prime Minister of New Zealand
Margo Dévai	Budapest, Hungary	Head of CHEF, a comprehensive health education foundation in Hungary
Jeanne Dukes	California	Educational Administrator, San Louis Obisbo County Office of Education
Ian Fox	Auckland, New Zealand	Middle school principal and Principal of the Year in New Zealand
Gavan Flick	Sydney, Australia	Owner and operator of Gevalia, an aboriginal art gallery
Ross Gilbert	Sydney, Australia	Associate Dean and head of teacher education, Sydney Conservatory of Music
Donald Gwira	Accra, Ghana	Communications Director, West African Division of Sight Savers International
Nola Hambleton	New Zealand	Principal and President of an international principal's association
Roger Harmon	Bangkok, Thailand	Director of Peace Corps, Thailand
Denese Henare	Auckland, New Zealand	Lawyer and community leader in the Maori tradition
Don Hazelwood	Sydney, Australia	Concertmaster for the Sydney Symphony Sydney Opera House, and First Violinist
John Hood	New Zealand	Vice-chancellor, Oxford University, former Vice-chancellor, Auckland Univ.

Figure I.1   Thrity–Six Exemplary Leaders

Name	Location	Position and Role
Bob Knight	Cape Coral, Florida	CFO, Paul Homes Construction
Gabor Halmai	Budapest, Hungary	President of Soros Foundation, the largest private foundation in Hungary
Fanny Law	Hong Kong	Secretary of Education and Manpower and leader of educational reform
Julianne Lowe	New Zealand	Tour Director throughout New Zealand for AAT Kings
Frank Lukasavitz	Milwaukee, Wisconsin	Industrial Designer and founding father of the Milwaukee Institute of Art and Design
Mandy Macleod	Brussels, Belgium	Principal, St. John's International School, Brussels
Ulice Payne	Milwaukee, Wisconsin	Former General Manager, Milwaukee Brewers Baseball Team
CJ Nickerson	Seattle, Washington	Retired President/founder, Comprehensive Health Education Foundation
Kuami Pianim	Accra, Ghana	Chief Executive Officer, New World Investments Limited, an organization committed to rebuilding the Ghanaian economy
Gary Rasmussen	Hong Kong	Business Manager, Hong Kong International School
Christine Rodriquez	Milwaukee, Wisconsin	Vice President, Rockwell Automation
Patrick Sayne	Paso Robles, California	Superintendent of Paso Robles Schools
Brenda Schoonover	Brussels, Belgium	Former U.S. Ambassador to TOGO and Chief of Mission in Brussels
Beth Stevenson	Atlanta, Georgia	Director of Youth Development and Education, American Cancer Society
Richard Teerlink	Milwaukee, Wisconsin	Former CEO, Harley Davidson Corporation
Mechai Viraviadya	Bangkok, Thailand	CEO/founder, Population Development Association in Thailand, former Minister of Health and Welfare for Thailand
Leotis Watson	Atlanta, Georgia	Head Concierge for the Emory Conference Center in Atlanta, Georgia

Figure I.1   Thrity–Six Exemplary Leaders (Continued)

motivation was a compelling interest in discerning universal leadership themes across diverse cultures and contexts. There was further interest in developing structures that would facilitate leaders' reflection about their leadership formation, performance, and sustainability. With those purposes in mind, the story lines of this book were organized around a compatible interview protocol.

Given the disparate roles and locations of the leaders drafted for this investigation, direct and long-term observation of their leadership behavior was not possible. Instead, interviews were employed to explore and interpret the nature of their leadership experience. As Patton (1991) explained:

> We interview people to find out from them those things we cannot directly observe: feelings, thoughts and intentions. We cannot observe behaviors that took place at some previous point in time. We cannot observe situations that preclude the presence of an observer. We cannot observe how people have organized the world and the meanings they attach to what goes on in the world. We have to ask people questions about those things. The purpose of interviews, then, is to allow us to enter into the other person's perspective. (p. 196)

To engage 36 leaders in reflection about how they influenced others toward the achievement of goals—and what formed and sustained their leadership capacity to do so—an interview protocol of three simple questions was devised:

1. What formed you as a leader?

2. What characterizes your performance as a leader?

3. What sustains you as a leader?

Siedman (1998) suggested that "at the root of in-depth interviewing is an interest in understanding the experiences of other people and the meaning they make of that experience" (p. 3). To that end, each of the participating leaders was asked to make meaning of their leadership experience in an interview that lasted from 1½ to 2 hours.

Although the interviews were structured for 90 minutes, most lasted nearly 2 hours. The interviewed leaders often started by saying they didn't think they had an hour's worth of things to say about their leadership; yet, once tapped, each leader found his or her reservoir of experience and insight to be deep and complex. Beyond the three main questions asked, prompts and cues were provided when necessary (see Figure 2).

Interestingly, in most cases, few prompts were needed in the interviews. In fact, it often appeared that a pent-up desire to reflect on their leadership experience motivated the leaders to converse at length in their response to each of the primary questions. Many became emotionally involved in telling their story, and laughter, tears, and lump-in-the-throat emotions were often evoked in the description of their lifelong vocations. Frequently, gratitude was

1. Leadership Formation: How did you come to leadership?

   Prompts:

   - What significant relationships, events, or other experiences influenced your journey to leadership?
   - What formal and/or informal preparation was valuable to your leadership development?

2. Leadership Performance: How do you conduct your leadership?

   Prompts:
   - What motivates/drives your leadership?
   - How do you see yourself as a leader?
   - What does your leadership look like to others?
   - How do you influence others toward the achievement of goals?

3. Leadership Sustainability: How do you sustain your leadership?

   Prompts:
   - How do you sustain results?
   - How do you sustain yourself?

Figure I.2   Interview Protocol: Leadership Formation, Performance, and Sustainability

expressed at the end of the interview for the opportunity to reflectively share their story and, in the process, put some of the puzzle pieces together for the first time. The telling of the story, more often than not, became a powerful and revealing experience for interviewer and interviewee alike.

All interviews were recorded, transcribed, and aligned to field notes kept during the interview sessions. Both the transcriptions and field notes were then analyzed to discern salient themes about leadership formation, performance, and sustainability. The themes that emerged from the analysis were organized around the interview questions that solicited insight about leadership formation, performance, and sustainability.

Given the nature of qualitative interviews, regardless of data quantity and quality, subjectivity of interpretation within the uniqueness of social settings and small samples limits generalizability to the greater population (Alvesson, 1996). Accordingly, the first three story lines of *Leading Coherently* relate observations about leadership formation, performance, and sustainability that are unique to the 36 interviewed leaders. Those stories are also formatted, however, for active reader participation in chapter conversations through a series of reflection exercises. A fourth story line then provides a culminating analysis across the first three, thus presenting a framework by which leaders might reflectively explore greater coherency within their leadership perception and practice. A brief preview of the four story lines follows.

LEADERSHIP FORMED

Part I of *Leading Coherently* opens with conversation about how a core of values and commitment is formed in leaders. It is a formation conversation about where leaders come from, that is, how they understand and embrace a call to lead.

Chapter 1 begins the conversation with brief profiles of 36 individuals who have demonstrated leadership success in diverse contexts around the world. At the end of the chapter, to connect the conversation to your own context, you are invited to add your leadership profile to those of the 36 exemplars.

Chapter 2 delves further into the backgrounds of the exemplary leaders and, in the process, reinforces the position that leaders are formed, not born. Chapter content describes how 36 leaders benefited from repeated opportunities for (a) building and testing values through interactions with their environment and significant others and (b) making the most of challenges, experimenting with work, and finding opportunities to spread their wings. The further conversation structured at the end of the chapter invites reflection about the shaping of your core values and the influence of those values on your vocational calling.

Chapter 3 presents an account of how the shaping of values and pursuit of vocational callings progressed to leadership commitments. Chapter content relates how the leaders became deeply committed to vocational callings rooted in core values as they moved down their formation path and were subsequently compelled to assume aligned leadership roles. Chapter 3 also describes a coherency—a logical and consistent relationship of values and purpose—within the leaders' formation experiences.

The further conversation structured at the end of the chapter solicits reflection about how you were prepared for and compelled to accept leadership responsibilities.

LEADERSHIP PERFORMED

Part II carries *Leading Coherently* forward to a conversation about leadership performance. That conversation focuses on the "how" of leadership. It is an account of how leaders conduct the leadership business of influencing others toward the achievement of goals. Within the conversation, Chapters 4 through 7 present a story of extended leadership coherence—a harmony between what 36 leaders professed to value, be, and do. It is a story that captures how, in the minds of the interviewed leaders, performance was strongly aligned to values and purpose, both in character and behavior. It is also an account about how force of character across prominent fields of behavior forged essential leadership connections to human capacity for growth and achievement.

Chapter 5 shares the interviewed leaders' accounts of performance that was humble, passionate, and contemplative in character. Chapter content also invites your reflection about character traits that define and influence your leadership performance.

Chapter 6 examines the alignment of values and character to three prominent fields of leadership behavior—community building, centering, and thinking—as described by 36 leaders. The conversation at the end of the chapter facilitates reflection about the relationship between your core values and prominent leadership behaviors.

Chapter 7 observes how the interviewed leaders' performance character and behavior established influential connections to others that were prominently social, emotional, and reflective in nature. Your participation in this end-of-chapter conversation will focus on your cultivation of social, emotional, and reflective dimensions of human capacity in yourself and your organization.

LEADERSHIP SUSTAINED

Part III of *Leading Coherently* advances the conversation to an account of what 36 leaders thought mattered most in sustaining organizational capacity for achieving results. Chapters 8 and 9 also examine the relationship of the third important element of leadership coherence—that of sustainability—to leadership formation and performance.

The conversation in Chapter 8 relates how the leaders valued and cultivated productive dispositions in themselves and their organizations as a means to compound and expand their leadership influence.

Chapter 9 adds perspective about strategies leaders employ to sustain their mind, body, and spirit within demanding leadership contexts—most often while assailed by ubiquitous demands, distractions, and detractors. Notably, the leaders reveal a learned understanding of the linkage between fulfilling purpose and fueling intellectual, physical, and spiritual needs. Their interest in personal maintenance, moreover, was not primarily concern for self, but rather for the consequence and legacy of their leadership.

Chapters 8 and 9 conclude with reflective exercises that facilitate review of your leadership attention to productive dispositions and how you might best sustain yourself in body, mind, and spirit.

LEADERSHIP LEARNED

Part IV synthesizes lessons progressively gleaned from Chapters 1 through 9 in Parts I through III. With reference to the wisdom shared by the interviewed leaders, this final portion of *Leading Coherently* conducts a summary review and a culminating reflection.

Chapter 10 describes the elements and relationships of "coherent leadership" as they emerged from the stories of 36 exemplary leaders. This description includes a model of leadership coherence that has implications for both understanding and facilitating the relationships between formation, performance, and sustainability within effective leadership. It is a model that interprets a dynamic and reciprocal relationship among the following elements: clarity of value and purpose, congruent character and behavior, compounded capacity, and resulting expansion of consequence.

Chapter 11 closes the leadership conversation organized within this book with examination of how that conversation might be extended. Chapter content invites your use of the model as a means to systematically reflect on your leadership formation, performance, and sustainability, and the extent of your own leadership coherence. To that end, additional strategies and practices for facilitating self and group reflection about the phenomenon of leadership are proposed. The final reflection in this chapter, of course, is one of deciding your next steps toward sustaining reflective leadership conversations and practice.

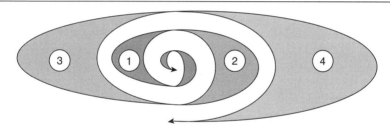

1. Leadership *formation* forges an inner coherence of core values, vocational calling, and commitment to lead.

2. An inner coherence about values, callings, and commitments is subsequently extended through congruent leadership *performance* aligned to the nature of human capacity.

3. A coherency between elements of leadership formation and performance is further extended to leadership *sustainability* through dispositions and strategies that elevate leadership influence.

4. A dynamic coherency between the elements of leadership formation, too loose performance, and sustainability expands leadership *consequence*.

Figure I.3   A Model of Coherent Leadership

Part I

Leadership Formed

The servant leader is servant first . . . It begins with the natural feeling that one wants to serve, to serve first. Then conscious choice brings one to aspire to lead.

–Robert Greenleaf (1996, p. 7)

The first three chapters of *Leading Coherently* describe how 36 exemplary leaders were shaped, called, committed, and compelled toward the assumption of leadership responsibilities. Drawing from personal reflection about their path to leadership, the leaders reveal fundamental elements of leadership formation—revelations that portray leaders who were formed, rather than born.

1

Exemplary Formations

You need robust dialogue to surface the realities of the business.

—Bossidy & Charan (2002, p. 23)

Profiles

It is natural to learn from example, whether good or bad. Given a choice, however, we most often turn to the positive rather than the negative—if for no other reason than to avoid the distress and disappointment associated with things done poorly. Learning from success also holds an edge over learning from mistakes because we associate expertise with things done well. That said, this inquiry opted to engage in reflective conversation with leaders who were reputed exemplars of effective leadership.

Because their stories form the backbone of the leadership conversations that unfold in the following chapters, a brief introduction to the cast of story-tellers is presented here. Short biographical profiles provide perspective on the collective leadership experience that was engaged in reflective conversation.

GOVERNMENT LEADERS

Michael Barber, Chet Bradley, Prime Minister Helen Clark, and Fanny Law were influential, reform-minded government officials. They were widely recognized for making an impact on their state or country's policies in a manner that enriched the quality of life for the populations they represented.

Michael Barber developed a strong desire to contribute to the greater good from his early Quaker roots in England. An educator by training, Michael communicated his philosophy of education in a book titled *The Learning Game.* When Tony Blair was running for prime minister, Michael was asked to articulate the candidate's platform for educational reform. Since then, Michael has served as lead policy analyst and advisor in the Labor government not only for education, but also for transportation and health care. As Director of the Prime Minister's Delivery Unit, he influenced the environment that affected his nation's children, as well as the educational system they experienced.

Chet Bradley hailed from a rural Wisconsin farm family in the midwestern United States. He liked to joke about his name: "Can you imagine someone looking into a crib and saying, 'Let's name him Chester'?" As a young athlete and health buff, he started his career teaching physical education and history. He was later transformed by a powerful learning experience in an innovative master's degree program in leadership at the University of Oregon. His resulting knowledge and skill, combined with a strong commitment to healthy kids and healthy schools, led him to a leadership position in health education at the Wisconsin Department of public Instruction.

Helen Clark grew up in rural New Zealand in the home of conservative parents. Recognized early for her intellect, she was sent to boarding school in Auckland as a young preteen. She formed strong values about fairness and access to opportunity that drove her to eventual leadership in the country's labor party. After a long and outspoken career in parliament, Helen was the first elected female to hold office as the Prime Minister of New Zealand. She also enjoyed the reputation of being the most results-oriented prime minister in New Zealand's history.

Fanny Law spent her early childhood in a crowded apartment in Hong Kong along with her seven siblings and a father who instilled a strong work ethic and high expectations. Finding a career in public service allowed her to serve and protect the rights of the people of Hong Kong. As a Chinese woman in a British-controlled protectorate, Fanny was in the unique position to help negotiate the return of Hong Kong to Chinese rule in 1999. As the Secretary of education and Manpower, Fanny used her influence to transform the Hong Kong education system toward a better investment in the community's youth and Hong Kong's future.

NONPROFIT ORGANIZATION LEADERS

Margo Dévai, Gabor Halmai, CJ Nickerson, and Mechai Viraviadya led nonprofit organizations that were mostly self-created. They worked on changing systems from the outside—with all the freedom and inventiveness that their outsider status allowed.

Margo Dévai spent most of her life and early career under the constraints of communist Hungary. Her family survived multiple hardships and, as a young woman, Margo learned to "hide her light under a bushel" and avoid leadership responsibilities. Slowly and reluctantly, she stepped up to lead as a university teacher dedicated to the creation of self-esteem in young children. As a result of her research, persistence, and the opportunity for self-determination after the demise of communism, Margo found herself leading a nonprofit Comprehensive Health Education Foundation that positively impacted teachers and students throughout Hungary.

Gabor Halmai presented a case for being the most extreme workaholic in the sample—a significant distinction considering the competition. Driven by his passion for social justice, he held not one but three demanding leadership roles in the emerging democracy of Hungary. Having suffered the ravages of Eastern European anti-Semitism early in his life and career, Gabor dedicated his life to the law and the rights and freedoms that post-communist Hungary had to offer. His role as President of the Soros Foundation in Hungary offered him the opportunity to provide resources for initiatives that supported human rights.

CJ Nickerson, a self-described American entrepreneur, left the confines of state department bureaucracy to build a private foundation that would fuel the health promotion and education efforts he valued. As a leader who always had the ability to "figure it out," he used his creativity and perseverance to leverage health education products into a self-sustaining Comprehensive Health Education Foundation with an endowment of over 30 million dollars. His innovative organization made a real difference in the development of healthy lifestyles for children in the state of Washington and throughout the country.

Mechai Viraviadya, better known as the "Condom King" in Thailand, made his initial impact on the welfare of his countrymen as Minister of Health by promoting population control. He led the fight against AIDS in a country that claimed one of the highest growth rates of the deadly disease through his creative and playful promotion of the condom. As a result, Thailand became one of the first countries to reverse the rising tide of the spread of HIV. Born of a Thai father and British mother, Mechai learned what it meant to be "the deviant" in early childhood and used those insights to advantage as he successfully built his own nonprofit Population Development Association to continue the work of eradicating poverty in his homeland.

K–12 EDUCATION LEADERS

Tim Brighouse, Rod Chamberlain, Jeanne Dukes, Ian Fox, Nola Hambleton, Mandy Macleod, Gary Rasmussen, and Patrick Sayne were inventive educators committed to the success of all students and the teachers who serve them. They worked in public, private, and international schools.

Tim Brighouse might best be described as Albert Einstein on fast-forward. His wild-eyed, bushy-haired, and intense intelligence belied a deeply reflective nature, undergirded by a lifelong commitment to educational success for all children. As the Superintendent of Birmingham, the second largest school district in England serving over 100,000 students, Tim decried the fact that he would be forced to retire at the age of 65. Like most of the other leaders interviewed for this project, retirement was neither an appealing nor a rational orientation. As Tim put it, "How could you ever be done?"

Rod Chamberlain found his niche early as a leader in independent schools. Committed to high standards of excellence for himself and others, his Mennonite upbringing prepared him to accept challenge as the norm and creative solutions as the natural outcome. As the headmaster of the Kamehameha School in Maui, Hawaii, Rod was charged with carrying on a seventh-generation vision held for Hawaiian students by the granddaughter of King Kamehameha himself: to build the first complete K–12 campus beyond the original school campus on Oahu.

Jeanne Dukes exuded a passion for serving those off the norm, that is, kids and adults who didn't fit the typical mold in public schooling. As an educational administrator for San Luis Obispo County Office of Education in California, Jeanne devoted her time and energy to the creation, staffing, and success of programs for at-risk students. As someone who came late to leadership after raising a family and starting a second career, Jeanne brought a full-time commitment to championing the rights of students who lacked advocates. She was also committed to supporting the "quirky" teachers who worked with such students on a daily basis.

Ian Fox was a study in perseverance. As a principal in the same middle-level school in Auckland for 14 years, he and his staff developed a prototype for student portfolios that became a national model in New Zealand. Ian believed that successful schools formed around a catalyst that bound school and community toward a common goal. The creation and execution of a comprehensive student assessment system provided just such focus for his school. As long as the direction was sound, the results were promising, and the task was unfinished, Ian intended to stay and see it through.

Nola Hambleton had gone beyond the typical school principalship to provide leadership for an international principals' association. As one of the first female principals in New Zealand, Nola was accustomed to blazing new paths for herself and for the organizations she led. Not satisfied with having an impact at the local level alone, she became the president of an international principals' association to provide a network of support for leaders such as herself.

Mandy Macleod intended to move from Scotland to Belgium for a year or two, but stayed for 30 years. As the successful headmaster of the middle school at St. John's International School in Waterloo, Mandy was known as a culture builder and nurturer in her school. Teachers spoke of her with fondness and trust, acknowledging that her door was always open no matter what level of need they expressed. With an eye always trained on student success, Mandy believed that her job as headmaster was to support St. John's teachers and empower them to do their jobs well.

Gary Rasmussen was an anomaly in the school business sector. Rather than being "Mr. No," as many business managers are often perceived, Gary viewed his role as that of facilitator of organizational mission. Using creative problem solving and an orientation toward stakeholder involvement, Gary operationalized the mission at Hong Kong International School through the deployment of targeted resources. Devoted to both his school and his family, Gary was a leader who worked hard to find and achieve a healthy balance between work and home life.

Patrick Sayne's experience and tenacity as a school superintendent belied the twinkle in his eye and wry smile on his lips. Using self-deprecating humor to demystify the role of "top dog" in Paso Robles School District in central California, Patrick's perspective was both realistic and idealistic. After 24 years in the superintendency in various districts, he invested his mental and emotional energy in the long view to minimize the day-to-day setbacks. As Patrick noted, "There's always another day."

PUBLIC HEALTH LEADERS

Alex Banful, Donald Gwira, and Beth Stevenson served organizations dedicated to the promotion of public health. They pursued their work as leaders of nonprofit agencies dedicated to health education and discovery of effective treatment and cures.

Alex Banful articulated a commitment that he lived out daily as the CEO of a nonprofit public health organization in Ghana, West Africa. Having left the private sector 10 years earlier, Alex had built the Ghana Social Marketing Foundation, a successful nongovernment organization that provided resources for AIDS and malaria prevention while also addressing other pressing health issues in rural areas of his country. Alex worked a relentless schedule, fueled by an entrepreneurial spirit and a drive to eradicate diseases dangerous to his fellow Ghanaians.

Donald Gwira was among the youngest leaders in the group of 36, a "30-something" man who was already making his mark as Communications Officer for a multinational health organization called Sight Savers International. As communications expert, he led the public relations effort across West Africa to get the word out about the prevention and cure of blindness. His creativity and "way with words" was effective in making the gift of sight a high priority for those within the reach of his information campaigns.

Beth Stevenson mixed creativity, risk taking, and humor in everything she did. As the oldest of three independent girls, Beth looked to her mother and grandmother as role models of strong professional women. Luckily, Beth found an avenue for channeling her energy into a profession that blended her twin passions, education and health promotion. As Director of Childhood

Cancer Prevention and Programs at the American Cancer Society, Beth created, supported, and sustained innovative programs that demonstrated real results in health promotion programs for children.

FOREIGN SERVICE LEADERS

Brenda Schoonover served as a foreign diplomat, building bridges of understanding across cultures and amid conflict. Similarly, Roger Harmon served his country as Director of the Peace Corps in Thailand.

Brenda Schoonover was a model of humility as a leader. After serving as Ambassador to Togo, Brenda was asked to come out of retirement to support the new Ambassador to Brussels as the Chief of Mission. Her experience and sound judgment were invaluable to that ambassador's transition from a business career, with little experience in international affairs, to diplomat. Her lifelong commitment to represent her country and willingness to put duty before self epitomized her leadership calling.

Roger Harmon was afflicted with an adventuresome spirit that landed him in Thailand for over two decades. As Director of Peace Corps in Bangkok, Roger supported the volunteers who provide aid and assistance in the villages of rural areas. By staying connected to the needs of those served and those providing the service, Roger led authentically and realistically.

JUSTICE SYSTEM LEADERS

Richard Bissen defended and protected the public safety of his county with a gentle but firm administration of the law. As a civil rights attorney, Denese Henare committed her career to securing equal rights for native Maori in New Zealand.

Richard Bissen was District Attorney of Maui County when interviewed and is now the First Deputy Attorney General for the State of Hawaii in Honolulu. He is the first native Hawaiian to achieve such rank in the justice system in his state. Richard reflected a laid-back and fun-loving nature often associated with his culture, but his deep commitment revealed a serious determination to protect his fellow Hawaiians, native or not. Within minutes of meeting him, people experienced a deep sense of trust and security that conveyed the assurances of a newfound friend.

Denese Henare was a fighter. As an attorney with Maori roots, she dedicated herself to the preservation of Maori rights guaranteed in New Zealand's Waitanga Treaty. In the Maori culture, it is said that women carry the tribal wisdom. As a result of her cultural heritage and legal training, Denese felt a deep sense of responsibility for ensuring the fair and equitable treatment of her kin and the best interests of her homeland.

HOSPITALITY INDUSTRY LEADERS

Julianne Lowe and Leotis Watson literally led to serve in the hospitality industry, giving care and attention to the weary tourist and harried traveler.

Julianne Lowe had eyes that sparkled with humor and mischievousness, qualities necessary to her success as a director for AAT King in New Zealand. Her patience, "people sense," and positive outlook on life were part disposition and part skill, developed early in her career as a nurse. She later used these skills to support and "shepherd" tourists around her beautiful country. Julianne's self-proclaimed goal was to help others discover the beauty and diversity of her native land, while at the same time renewing her own sense of wonder on a regular basis.

Leotis Watson "owned" the lobby of the Emory Conference Center in Atlanta, Georgia. When a customer stepped inside, he was there to serve the person's every need. As the head concierge supervising 25 employees, Leotis was a success story of the first order. Having survived a period of homelessness in San Francisco, Leotis's belief in himself and a god-given duty to help others propelled him to become a successful model and leader within his niche in the hospitality industry.

HIGHER EDUCATION LEADERS

John Hood and Ross Gilbert provided leadership in the most intransigent of all institutions, that is, higher education, and they did so with remarkable success and aplomb.

John Hood was selected "Man of the Year" by a prominent New Zealand magazine for his success as a businessman who made the transition to university administration. As Vice Chancellor of the University of Auckland, John successfully bridged the gap between the private and public sectors, making a notable impact as a leader in both. Referencing core beliefs to guide practice in both arenas, John's clear focus, articulate vision, and strong faith in the capabilities of others helped to make a real difference in the life of the university and the university's relationship with the greater Auckland community.

Ross Gilbert was a professor who gave higher education a good name. As Director of Music Education for the Sydney Conservatory of Music, Ross had lived and breathed teacher preparation for over 30 years. Mixing the power of relationships with the science of research, Ross developed a successful, cutting edge program that turned musicians into teachers—no small feat. With an office located in the midst of the Sydney Botanical Gardens, Ross uses his surroundings to facilitate reflection on practice, for himself and his students.

CORPORATE LEADERS

Corporate sector leaders included Boon Yoon Chiang, CEO of multinational Jardine-Matheson in Singapore; Bob Knight, CFO for the Florida-based

Paul Homes construction company; Ulice Payne, General Manager for the Milwaukee Brewers baseball team; Kuami Pianim, CEO of a Ghanaian investment firm; Christine Rodriguez, a Vice President for Rockwell Automation in Milwaukee, Wisconsin; and Rich Teerlink, former CEO of Harley-Davidson Motorcycles.

Boon Yoon Chiang expressed himself with a gentle smile and soft-spoken humility. Such humility was all the more notable, given his position as CEO of Jardine-Matheson, the largest trading company in Singapore, a company that employed over 6,000 people. Yoon Chiang began his career as a journalist where he honed the social skills that were later used in building business relationships. His keen "people sense" allowed him to hire and nurture well-matched employees. His faith in the worth of employees promoted investment in their success and, in turn, gained their commitment to the mission of Jardine-Matheson.

Bob Knight was brought into the fledgling Paul Homes construction corporation to grow the business to the next level. That he did. Paul Homes became a large, award-winning home construction company in southwest Florida under Bob's visionary and collaborative leadership. Characteristically positive in his outlook, Bob saw potential in every employee and felt personally responsible for insuring employee success commensurate with the success of the company.

Ulice Payne aspired to live his commitments and embody his core values. As a product of a small steel town on the banks of the Allegheny, where open-hearth furnaces ran 24/7, Ulice learned that leadership was about "showing up" and being himself. True to his nature, he was known for taking an ethical stance when decisions were tough and results hung in the balance.

Kuami Pianim personified courage in the face of adversity and faith in the future. A successful corporate leader and social activist, Kuami was imprisoned for 10 years as a political foe of one of the former military regimes in Ghana. Ever a populist, Kuami fought to preserve human rights and dignity, even while in prison. On his release, he became a leading candidate for his country's presidency until the reigning president ordered a constitutional amendment to restrict "ex-convicts" from becoming state officials. Undaunted, Kuami formed New World Investments Ltd, with the mission of building the economy of his impoverished, developing country.

Christine Rodriguez was the first Latina to hold a significant executive position at Rockwell Automation. As Vice President for State and Community Relations, she was the face of Rockwell in the greater community. Her job was to enhance the image of the company as a good corporate citizen. As she noted, "The community where the company lives and works gives the business license to operate. It is our job to help maintain a balanced community. This is a legacy that I take very seriously."

Rich Teerlink helped put Harley-Davidson Motorcycles on the map. A self-effacing leader, Rich was disposed to credit others for his own remarkable accomplishments. Accessible, open, and committed to "giving back," Rich exemplified faith in others and the power of teams to solve their own problems and create their own destiny. As a result, his unified business philosophy is studied in management programs around the world.

FINE AND APPLIED ARTS LEADERS

Three gentlemen of diverse interests and experiences represented the arts. Gavan Flick was an art dealer who created and operated the first and only Aborigine-owned art gallery in Sydney. Don Hazelwood, also from Australia, was a gifted violinist who rose to the status of concertmaster for the Sydney Symphony. Frank Lukasavitz was an industrial designer and founder of a premier postsecondary art school in Milwaukee, Wisconsin.

Gavan Flick was a success story in a land that often withheld success from those of aboriginal descent. Through grit and determination, he dedicated his life to the preservation of aboriginal art and support for budding young Aborigine artists. His hard-won success was apparent in the stylish Gavala gallery he opened in the Stanley Marketplace in an upscale section of Sydney, Australia. True to his commitment, profits from artwork sales were shared and invested beyond the usual gallery-artist arrangements to further encourage the endeavors of Aborigine artists.

Don Hazelwood just wanted to be the best violin player he could be. In the process, he became the first chair of the Sydney Symphony, which included the responsibilities of concertmaster. That job entailed leadership navigation of issues and procedures between the conductor and the rest of the orchestra. Don's commitment to the orchestra compelled his successful service in that role for many years.

Frank Lukasavitz was cofounder of one of the top five design schools in America. Following his early success as an industrial designer, Frank worked with several colleagues to create an art school that would promote and develop applied arts in the Midwest. Thirty years later, the Milwaukee School of Art and Design was one of the best-known and highest-ranked art schools in the United States. Well past retirement age for most people, Frank still taught at the Milwaukee Institute for Art and Design out of love for his students and his commitment to the field.

Further Conversation

With reference to the profiles, this is an appropriate moment for you to introduce yourself as the 37th participant in the leadership conversations that will unfold over the next 10 chapters. The following reflection exercise will assist you to that end.

EXERCISE 1.1   Further Conversation: Leadership Profile

In the space below, write a brief leadership profile of yourself that describes you by:

A. Name:

B. Geographical Location:

C. General Biographical Information:

D. Leadership Experience:

E. Leadership Passions and Achievements:

2

Values and Calling

No longer is it nature versus nurture but nature via nurture. Genes are designed to take their cues from nurture.

—Ridley (2003, pp. 3–4)

Shaped

The debate about whether leaders are born or made is an old one. One position has historically maintained that leadership is an inborn gift, like the acute coordination of a natural athlete or the perfect pitch of an exceptional musician. The other side of the argument proposes that leadership is a skill shaped by life experience.

Fortunately, scientific discovery is progressively putting such polarized arguments about nature versus nurture to rest. Breakthrough knowledge emanating from neuroscience and the biotechnical unraveling of the human genome has been particularly helpful to settling the debate. Such discoveries have established that virtually all human qualities are the product of rich and complex interactions between nature and nurture. We each come into this world endowed with a biological package born of our unique genetic legacy. But we also know that the environment in which we are nurtured has a tremendous effect on how our package will unfold and prosper. Simply put, there is a necessary and magical interplay between genetic endowment and the cumulative effect of environmental interactions with people, places, and other experiences over a lifetime.

FORMED MORE THAN BORN

Accepting the interactive influence of nature and nurture on human development in general, one might nevertheless question the weight of nurture on the development of any particular quality. Returning to the debate about whether leaders are born or made, for example, one might inquire as to how important nurture is to the emergence of leadership qualities. That is, given that nature provides the essentials of a healthy body and mind, a question remains as to what degree and in what manner nurture unlocks and advances leadership potential in individuals.

> "My parents were very clear that you were on the planet to make a difference."
>
> —Michael Barber

An answer to that question emerges from the 36 leaders interviewed for this study. Their life experiences, as shared through their stories, suggest that leaders are much more formed than born.

That leaders are strongly formed by life experience is further accented by the revelation that leadership was never a primary goal for any of the 36 interviewed leaders. Rather, they were nurtured by early life experiences toward the formation of core values that anticipated vocational callings and, ultimately, a commitment to lead. In this fashion, the formation of a coherent leadership model begins to emerge. It is a model that is founded on values initially shaped by family and community, cultural context, and mentor influence.

FORMED BY FAMILY AND COMMUNITY

Our childhood environment is an obvious early influence on how we understand and engage in the world. You might observe, for example, that the values you hold today are traceable to the formative experiences of your past. Whether you express respect for a great-grandmother's stoicism, admiration for a brother's courage, or disdain for a miserly aunt's austerity, you are almost certain to reflect the influence of early interactions with prominent people in your life.

> "I grew up in a small town during the years when it was still a segregated society. Halethope was a small African American community that was very stable. A lot of the people in the community were relatives or married to relatives, so it was a very nurturing community."
>
> —Brenda Schoonover

The phenomenon of family and community influence on leadership formation is very apparent within the stories shared by the 36 participants in the study. They all identified early relationships that contributed to their leadership formation. They described elaborate webs of connections with immediate and extended family, friends, and mentors.

Such experience contributed to the development of a richly textured core of values for each of the leaders. Their family roots and childhood experiences, within a cultural overlay, imprinted a strong moral foundation that oriented subsequent leadership commitment and behavior. An example of such moral orientation was the leaders' shared perception that they were put on this earth to make a contribution, not simply to take up space.

Reflection about strong familial influence, for better or worse, was usually where the interview conversation began. From Milwaukee to Hong Kong and Accra to Brussels, mothers and fathers appeared again and again as strong influences on the initial formation of core leadership values.

Richard Bissen, district attorney for Maui County at the time of the interview and now first deputy attorney general for the state of Hawaii, came from a large extended Hawaiian family. In addition to valuing equity and fairness, his family held expectations for a better future. Richard was quite the cut-up in his youth, loving parties, friends, and "heckling." He observed that his mother helped save him from himself by sharing high expectations and instilling a value for self.

> I give a lot of credit to my mom. I was closer to her. They [parents] both came from as poor of a background as you can imagine, but they gave me a great upbringing. . . . Everything was "work with what you have," and they made sacrifices for me. I learned that you could be as happy as you want to be. My mom's big advice to me was "don't get involved with girls, stay on track, you will be somebody someday."

From further across the Pacific, Mechai Viraviadya, Chairman of the Population and Community Development Association in Thailand and better known as the "Condom King" for his innovative work in population control and AIDS prevention, told of the strong, unwavering influence his mother had on the formation of his understanding of what was important in life.

> We were driving somewhere when I was a little boy. The car was at an inter-section and there was another car at the side. An old woman was crossing the street with a basket and she was slow. The other car tooted its horn to speed her up and my mother turned to me and said, "Look what a sad thing this is. . . . He's got the money to buy a car, she's old and should be resting at home, but she has to work. And here he is speeding her along. He ought to get out and help her." She taught me to be straightforward and honest and do some-thing to help other people whenever possible.

John Hood, Vice Chancellor of the University of New Zealand, told of an equally compelling relationship with his father.

> My father was principal of the school I attended and got special dispensation to keep me an extra year. . . . He taught me one on one . . . world history, English literature from Beowulf to the present, English grammar, mathemat-ics, and science. I had a fantastic year, really. It was very Socratic and had a large impact on my intellectual maturity. I think that was quite formative. I haven't really analyzed it too hard, but I suspect if one looks back, that was a changing point in my life.

From Africa, Alex Banful, directing founder of a nonprofit health agency in Ghana, described learning a strong sense of morality from his mother's actions and words.

> My brother went out shopping with my mother. She was paying for something and realized she had run out of money. My brother said, "Oh, I have it," and gave her some money. She said, "Where did you get this from?" He responded, "I found it." They got home and he received the spanking of his life. She said to him, "It wasn't yours, so why did you take it?" Her point was don't ever take something that wasn't given to you.

The values of hard work and responsibility were modeled for many leaders as they saw their parents put forth an extended effort in support of a family. Ulice Payne, former General Manager of the Milwaukee Brewers baseball team, recalled,

> I came up in what would now be called a low-income household. I didn't know it then, but my dad always worked two jobs and my mother worked as well. We never owned our home, never had a new car, never took a vacation. But my father was the commander of the American Legion Post and my mother was head of the women's auxiliary. I always seemed to be in situations helping my parents out, and they were always in leadership positions. Leadership is just what they did.

Familial ties combined with strong religious beliefs to imprint messages that lasted a lifetime. Rod Chamberlain, Headmaster of Kamehameha School in Maui, came from a family of school administrators and Mennonite ministers.

> I grew up in a family where leadership was expected. My father had been in administration in church and schools. Most of my uncles and grandfathers were ministers, so when we got together the conversation was always [about] what went on and how to make it better. It was just always there—all the time. At dinner conversations we would talk about church policy. Embedded in this was a sense of values and why you would want to make certain things happen.

Similarly, Quaker roots and parental values helped to form Michael Barber, Director of the Prime Minister's Delivery Unit in England.

> My parents were very clear that you were on the planet to make a difference. It was absolutely assumed that you were getting a good education and you were going to improve the lot of humanity. I'm very driven by that possibility and that opportunity. I really appreciate, benefit from, and try to live by the values and attitudes I learned from them. A key Quaker value is not treating people differently because of their status. The phrase is "There is that of God in every man," so I never have difficulty seeing people as people.

Of course, people in our lives can influence us both positively and negatively. Two examples spoke loudly for the impact of a negative parental influence as well as the will to escape its effects. Leotis Watson, Head Concierge of the Emory Conference Center in Atlanta, spoke at length about the damaging effect his parents' lack of recognition and encouragement had had on him and how it was counterbalanced by his desire to override it.

> Still today my parents have never said, "You turned out to be a decent person" or "You've done a great job." I always had a burning desire to be my own person and if I couldn't get it [encouragement] at home it was hard for me to believe it from others. But still, I always felt that I was going to make something out of my life. It was going to be turned around.

Jeanne Dukes, the Special Program's Director for Paso Robles California County School Consortium, found herself moving away from the message her father drummed into her psyche throughout childhood. Her father was a World War II veteran and had been a chaplain in the war.

> There was a lot of macho and religious stuff going on. Pretty overpowering. We had traditional parenting with my mother staying home and my father tilting at windmills. My father was very much the person who always knew everything. . . . As long as he was around, there was no point in discussing it further. Maybe it was in conjunction with his passing away that I found out my ideas weren't so stupid after all.

Through negative imprinting, both Jeanne and Leotis learned the value of positive reinforcement or, more accurately, the consequence of the lack thereof. They also learned the value of high expectations held for the self and others.

Ultimately, such family influence affected not only the formation of core values, but how such values would later be expressed, as Rich Teerlink, former CEO of Harley Davidson described.

> I grew up in a family where my dad was a tool and dye maker, my mother was a seamstress. Later in life my dad became an entrepreneur and started his own business. He believed that the people he was leading were very, very important. He really wanted to get their input and was always talking to people. That was a principle I always followed.

Whether in the form of role models and ideals to be emulated or negative influences to be overcome, family and communal experiences played an important role in the formation of the 36 leaders. Nascent values were emerging, ready to mature when given the opportunity.

FORMED BY CULTURAL CONTEXT

Each budding leader was immersed in the particular cultural context of his or her youth. Those contexts, of course, existed within the larger cultural influences of nation, ethnicity, and religion. But such influences are nevertheless most closely experienced through the more intimate culture of family and local community. Richard Bissen spoke with great passion about the impact of his Hawaiian upbringing.

> "In my lifetime, I have seen two independences in a sense: the Indonesian from the Dutch, and after that the self-governing state of Singapore. So it is interesting to experience this twice. It is good for you to be able to shape and control your own destiny. In a sense, that experience played a part in what I subsequently did."
>
> — *Boon Yoon Chiang*

Being a Hawaiian family, we had parties on the weekend. My uncle was in the catering business. The family would help with putting on luaus, so music and family and parties were part of my life. I have 65 cousins, and I was the first to graduate from college. I wouldn't intentionally do anything to embarrass my family's name. They have done so much for me. It would be the worst thing I could do.

Denese Henare, a lawyer and community leader from New Zealand, echoed the same sentiments about her experience growing up in the Maori tradition.

The elders in our community are valued for their wisdom, and the guardians of culture are the women. They are valued as repositories of knowledge and emulate a strong sense of service in their work within the Maori culture.

Freedom from domination by outside cultures had a strong influence on Donald Gwira, Communications Officer of Sight Savers International in Ghana, West Africa.

I was born in the era of the liberation movement in Africa with Dr. Kwame Nkrumah, Ghana's first president, leading that crusade. Nkrumah lived by his principles and died for them. . . . My father is an avowed Nkrumhaist and still swears by him. 'Til this day we both appreciate what Nkrumah did for mother Ghana and the African continent as a whole.

Gary Rasmussen, Business Manager for the Hong Kong International School, grew up in a Protestant farming family in rural Illinois, learning the value of a strong work ethic and sacrificing for the future. Because his childhood asthma was severe, his family left their roots and livelihood to remake a life in Arizona, where Gary could not only breathe easier but also thrive in an educational system perceived to be of higher quality. "From that point on, my parents stressed the importance of an education for my lifetime skills as opposed to working on the farm. That was a significant point in my life."

Similarly, Ulice Payne learned the values of hard work and tenacity built from the tough environment of steel town, America.

> I grew up in a small steel town, Donora, Pennsylvania, on the Allegheny River. The steel mill never closed because you can't shut the ovens off. People in the steel mills worked double shifts. There is a strong work ethic and a sense of grit in steelworkers. This is what you did and you did it well. The better you did it, the prouder you were.

The culture of the family unit itself influenced many dimensions of value development. Beth Stevenson, Director of Childhood and Youth Initiatives for the American Cancer Society, explained how a value for cleverness, creativity, and humor was imprinted.

> My family's culture is really strong. It has always valued doing things against the current, and creativity was always extremely reinforced. Our family stories are about when my sister got lost in the Grand Canyon, or when we took our Japanese foreign exchange student camping in the rain, or how we always roasted our Thanksgiving turkey outside in a state park over an open pit. . . . Being weird and a little quirky is part of the family culture. As a result, I was always good at throwing ideas out and troubleshooting with creativity.

Most of the 36 leaders articulated not only the contextual effect of their familial and wider communal cultures, but also the clear link to values they held in their adult lives. They learned value for family, relationships, and hard work, particularly the responsibility one holds for those who care for you and for whom you care. Service to others seemed to be thus ingrained as a lifelong responsibility. Through early life events, the leaders developed the value for sacrifice and putting the needs of others before self.

FORMED BY MENTORS

In Homer's *Odyssey,* the warrior Odysseus goes off to fight the Trojan wars and entrusts the guidance of his son Telemachus to his good friend, Mentor. Mentor protects and nurtures Telemachus, introduces him to other leaders, and helps guide his development. Borrowing from that ancient Greek mythology, a *mentor* is commonly defined today as a "wise and loyal advisor" or a " faithful guide, especially for a younger person; an intimate friend who is also a wise counselor" (American Heritage Dictionary, 2000). Morton-Cooper and Palmer (2000) suggest that the raison d'être for such mentoring includes the following:

> "A lot of people have been incredibly good mentors. There's probably a little bit of them in me."
>
> —John Hood

Building a dynamic relationship

Sharing, encouraging, and supporting practice

Nurturing a base of mutual attraction and common values

Enabling and cultivating another

Making the most of human potential

As one might expect, the 36 leaders came into contact with multiple mentors in their formative years, many of whom became valuable colleagues or lifelong friends. Their mentors served as guides, sources of feedback, role models, skill builders, liaisons, clarifiers, and even constructive criticizers. Additionally, and perhaps most importantly, mentors imbued or reinforced values and attitudes that lasted a lifetime.

Not surprisingly, the males often found strong role models in sports, schooling, and early career opportunities. Mechai Viraviadya found mentors in his teachers.

> The headmaster and the housemaster at school guided me. They were very good examples of integrity. I learned that if you are dishonest, you are not much of a person regardless of what you may have around you. If you do something wrong, you own up to it and take the consequences.

Michael Barber also turned to his teachers for guidance and support.

> I had two history teachers, one of whom also ran the cricket team. The first one just expected me to do very well and would say something if he thought I was falling below the standard he thought I should be aspiring to. The second one taught me to write well. He made me think about writing, and they gave me feedback with good humor in the kind of context that the Quaker school generally allows for equal respect in the relationship.

Michael and Mechai were grateful for their teacher-mentors and the influence they had through values modeled and ingrained. Teachers who stimulated thought about one's role in life similarly influenced Tim Brighouse's early thinking, as well as his later work as Superintendent of Birmingham Schools in England.

> I had some teachers at secondary school who were very good at speculating, at provoking thought and argument. One in particular was brilliant at it. He would articulate the issues of the day, and you could see that this person was changing how we saw the world by speculating about the big issues and our role in them and what we might do about them. The world was something that you affected and had to play a part in.

In addition to teachers, career mentors played a huge role for some of the leaders during their school and early career years. For Richard Bissen, it was a guest speaker who became a career model and guide.

> In my sophomore year we had a career day. I heard the deputy prosecuting attorney, Joe Cordoza. I became very inspired and set my mind right then and there [that] that is what I would be. I met Joe again as a senior and shadowed him for a day. I kept telling him what I wanted to do, and he would say first finish high school and later finish college. After law school, the person who inspired me hired me. Joe became my boss.

As an NBA basketball player, Ulice Payne found a career mentor who cautioned him to think about his future and what might be most important. "J. Bruce was one of my mentors. He reminded me to consider what I would do when the basketball was over. He didn't tell me what to do, but reminded me to think about it."

Even earlier in his basketball career, Ulice found a powerful role model in his Marquette University coach who imbued values that Ulice later espoused himself. "Al McGuire helped me. He was a leader in his field, very proud, demanding, self-motivated, and not afraid to be different."

For Patrick Sayne, a school district superintendent in California, an influential male advisor also made a difference.

> As a young teacher I saw many principals, and I really admired my third one, Ralph Hanna. He was a strong figure, but not dictatorial. He was a facilitator; you could talk to him. He recognized things before they became a problem and was a proactive leader. I took my administrative leadership training under him. I was a brash young man, and Ralph could channel my energy. Later in my career, I asked him, "How did you keep from slapping me sideways? I was such a smart ass." He just smiled. There was patience and wisdom in his mentoring.

Early skill development and thinking habits were nurtured through observing the finesse of established leaders. Ross Gilbert, teacher educator and Associate Dean of the Sydney Conservatory of Music, recalled a principal who imparted the drive for organization, professionalism, positivism, and doing things with class.

> He was the first really driven principal I had and really came to in-service his staff and open up staff meetings and made people feel comfortable to contribute. Staff meetings were more than where the garbage bins go, but how should we teach social studies. How do we develop their thinking skills? And he always wore a coat and tie, looked very smart, and he spoke beautifully at assemblies. He was always very positive with the kids. He was certainly a model for me, and I guess I'm still trying to emulate that.

CJ Nickerson, CEO and Founder of the Comprehensive School Health Foundation in Seattle, Washington, credits his own open and reflective nature to early career mentors who taught him the value of analytical thinking and hard work.

> Luceille Trecona was the state supervisor of health education when I first started out. As a young teacher, not understanding protocol, I dropped in unannounced to her office and she took the time to look me in the eye and listen to my aspirations for health education. She taught me that you should always have your door open to everyone, no matter their station in life. Her honesty, trustworthiness, intelligence, and commitment were a model for me. Later, Dr. Hal Conacia, a professor at the University of San Francisco, taught me the benefit of reflection. He would disagree with you one day and then come back in a day or two to pursue the idea further.

Outside of school and work, athletic mentors contributed to values development—sometimes by negative example. Roger Harmon, Director of Peace Corps Thailand, developed empathy from watching one coach obsess about the competitiveness of sports.

> [There was] one coach I did not like, he was so driven to be successful. He thought he was a good role model, but he based success on winning, winning, winning. I have reacted against that all of my life. The measures of success that I think are more important are sportsmanship, teamwork, fair play, [and] growth. I've always been very sensitive to fairness and inclusion.

Mentors come in groups as well. Gabor Halmai, President of the Soros Foundation in Hungary and a leader of Human Rights Watch, was drawn into a circle of friends in the opposition movement against communism. Through finding a home for his interests, he was reinforced in his ability to articulate his values.

> In the 80s, I had many friends in the opposition. It was a group of people, mostly journalists and academics, and we wanted to have an area where freedom of speech could work. We still meet and are still working on disturbing issues concerning free speech. These people for me are more than friends. This was one of the aspects that was very important for me.

Gary Rasmussen found himself in a highly collegial and caring group of school administrators early in his career.

> I would say another positive turning point was being part of a real collegial caring group of administrators. We all nurtured each other. Because I was going through a difficult family situation at the time, that was a really stabilizing

factor in my life. We all felt comfortable with each other and respected each other individually but also professionally.

While not the ideal, lessons are again nevertheless learned from negative mentor role models as well. Tim Brighouse related such an experience.

> The second head I worked for gave me all sorts of negative examples, like always double guessing you, always making you feel that whatever you did you should have done it better, losing the energy of the staff, and ducking out on difficult issues because he was essentially afraid. I knew I couldn't survive and couldn't stay there.

Many of the women interviewed expressed the power of other women as role models, supporters, and indispensable mentors in their formation. Such mentors came in the form of mothers, grandmothers, and role models in the workplace. Beth Stevenson described the impact of strong females in her early development.

> I had a sense of these strong, compassionate women with a lot of conviction and very strong opinions. . . . My mother was a middle-class mom with radical political views. My grandmother was an English teacher who had to drop out of medical school early in her life for financial reasons. She was an amazing woman who led a pre-Internet intellectual distance debate in the Unitarian Church, and was a one-woman Red Cross in her county who worked with migrant workers living in shacks during World War II to keep them informed about their sons in the service.

Brenda Schoonover, Chief of Mission in Brussels and former U.S. Ambassador to Togo, identified her mother as a powerful mentor influence in her life. "My mother is a very, very strong figure in my life. She was the stable, constant force. She was a big influence on me and let me take risks."

Julianne Lowe, a director for AAT King in New Zealand, described a similar perception of the strong influence emanating from her mother.

> Mom was never the weak little woman and dad was not the wimpy man that mom led. They both worked together and had a good partnership. Mom was ahead of her time. A woman of that era took second place, but she didn't and was very independent. All three of her girls are very independent as a result. She was a very good role model.

Nola Hambleton, a New Zealand principal, bridged her mother's influence to other strong female models.

> My mother was very keen on us doing what we wanted because she had given up her job when she married. There's a culture in New Zealand that you have

to be a man to be a principal. So the women principals I know, we all know that we had to work twice as hard to prove ourselves. One of my mentors was the first woman principal in Dunedin. She was wonderful. . . . She gave me the idea that you are the principal . . . [and to] get on with the job and don't dismiss your ability and worry about what people are saying. She was the most energetic and enthusiastic person right up to the end of her career.

These women learned from other women that they could be strong, smart, and effective in whatever they endeavored. Learning these lessons early in their lives instilled a keen affinity for such attributes as well as a sense that *they* could be strong, smart, and effective.

Called

Not to be confused with a job, which can be transient, a life calling provides an avenue for living out one's values. The formation stories of the 36 leaders all speak to the search, discovery, and successful embrace of such calling. Mechai Viraviadya, for example, held many different jobs in government and in the private and nonprofit sector, but always with strong value for equity of opportunity. His life's calling never wavered from "the eradication of poverty in Thailand." Gabor Halmai held three jobs at the time of his interview, but all three jobs served his life's calling "to insure and protect human rights in Hungary." His work allowed him to focus wholeheartedly on the value he held for serving others and upholding basic human dignity.

> Calling: A claim on a person's time or life; a strong inner urge or prompting; a vocation.
>
> —American Heritage Dictionary (2000)

Formulation of clear life callings occurred in many ways over time for all 36 of the interviewed leaders, but a few common factors surfaced as critical to such development. Specifically, there were salient patterns that described how the leaders were called to vocations through adversity, opportunity, and early work experience.

CALLED BY ADVERSITY

Many of the leaders talked about some form of adversity that affected them early in life. Such stories usually illustrated the development of inner strength and conviction. Through experiencing and surviving challenges, the leaders cultivated a reservoir of strength that could be later called on when most needed. Hardship further helped them to prioritize and decide what was really important in life in relation to their value formation. Ultimately, prior experience with distress developed a resiliency that the leaders could call on as they came up against the challenges of leadership.

Several of the leaders viewed themselves as outcasts or deviants within the wider society. This occurred mainly because of the cultural isolation caused by membership in a minority race, religion, or culture. Experiencing prejudice, ostracism, or hatred left its mark. Mechai Viraviadya was mindful of the influence of his minority status.

> "My family had many, many bad events in their lives. We lost everything twice. The first was during the Second World War. We lived in Budapest and the bombs destroyed everything. With the changeover to communism, my father couldn't work in the new government. We had to keep my family's past a big secret so that I could go to the university."
>
> —Margo Dévai

> I was a deviant in society. Being of Thai and Scottish origin made me a minority of one, and in Thai culture this was a problem. I knew that I had to learn to be flexible and pay very close attention. Having experienced that led to my focus on equal rights and resources for all.

Brenda Schoonover shared a similar perspective of what was worth fighting for from her experience with gender discrimination.

> I grew up in a segregated society, so prejudice was beginning to come out in other forms that I hadn't thought about. They didn't want to put me in a house in the Peace Corps because I was a woman. I finally had a meeting with the country director and said this has got to stop. Later I had to fight not only for housing but for equitable job responsibilities. I learned from these experiences to be firm and direct.

For both Mechai and Brenda, their experiences with adversity coupled with their core values. Such experience eventually led to their selecting career paths in health care and diplomacy, respectively. For both, the value for human worth became a focus of their calling. Similarly, Gabor Halmai revealed that the prejudice he experienced in his early years as a Jew in Eastern Europe caused him to be passed up for promotion, thus solidifying his interest in human rights.

> After finishing the university, I felt that I was treated incorrectly. I wasn't accepted at the university as an assistant at the law school. I had to go over to the University of Budapest and teach constitutional law. I always had the feeling that I [was] not accepted by a part of my field. I think that is partly because of anti-Semitism in Hungary. The law school almost never accepted Jews as professors. This drove me to show that I am better than them.

Denese Henare ended up devoting her life to land rights when she came to understand the prejudice against Maori in New Zealand and the subtle and not so subtle forms of domination they endured.

I have lived in a culture of domination. I was the first Maori woman to graduate in law from Auckland University. When I took constitutional law, I realized that there was nothing in the course about Maori land law. My work is to combine British common law and Maori culture as two streams, creating law that speaks with a New Zealand accent. My work is focused on understanding the values and meanings within certain contexts so that our institutions are more sensitive to Maori beliefs and traditions.

For some, adversity arrived through the normal pangs of adolescence. The difference was in how they chose to deal with it, as Ulice Payne illustrates.

I used to be a skinny, pimply-faced kid, and girls didn't like me. I think I got into a lot of things because I wasn't a romantic kind of guy. As a young child, 5 years old until about 8, I had respiratory problems. I couldn't go outside on certain hot days with the steel mill's pollution. I would go out on the porch with my grandma and string green beans and comb her hair. I found that I had time to do other things. . . . I spent a lot of time alone, dreaming, wishing.

After a while, such adversity and isolation led to an inner certainty and trust in Ulice's values and opinions that paid off later in life.

When you're young you need so much confirmation, but there came a point where I didn't worry about confirmation. I would think, "I know you don't like me anyway. I know you're laughing at me anyway. I'm skinny or sickly." So I didn't worry about fitting in because I didn't fit in. My brother was smart and handsome. So I evolved on my own and didn't worry about the opinion of anyone else. It became much less relevant what other people thought. If I thought it was the best thing to do, then I just did it. Over time I looked around and found that everyone is following.

Leaders who were born to dominant or privileged culture or class were also influenced by encounters with injustice. CJ Nickerson, a white male in America, observed prejudice while in high school and was affected by the experiences of his African American friends.

I was invited to join a HI-Y, which was a high school fraternity with status. But I noticed that my friends, many of whom were of color, were not allowed to join. Rather than join myself, I came up with the idea of creating a club in our town that was more inclusive. We got the help of a local African American leader who helped us formalize and legitimize our club. I learned that you don't have to accept the status quo!

Beyond prejudice and isolation, challenge came in other forms. Being uprooted from the comforts of home was another common experience shared by many of the 36 leaders. Whether because of an early family move in their life or because they were sent to boarding school, many learned early lessons about who they were and what they stood for. While boarding school was the necessary track for a quality education in their respective cultures, it came at a cost for Boon Yoon Chiang, CEO of Jardine-Matheson in Singapore, and Helen Clark, Prime Minister of New Zealand. Boon Yoon Chiang described the impact boarding school had on the development of his resolve.

> I came here when I was very young and on my own. I was twelve. I went to a boarding school and had to learn to be independent and look after myself. Whether you like it or not, you have to. I had to build character.

Helen Clark also referenced her resiliency to an experience with boarding school. "I was sent to boarding school from a small farming community to the big city of Auckland at the age of 13. That's where I developed resiliency."

Several leaders were uprooted by family moves during formative and vulnerable ages. Jeanne Dukes shared one such story that caused her to sort out what was important and what was not.

> We had a pretty good standard, middle-class Midwestern life until he [father] annoyed one too many people, the president of the college he was working for at the time. This was very disruptive. We had to leave Iowa and move to southern California. I was 15. It was really awful. That taught me that life was not fair and you can't fix some things. You have to be tough. I came from a sheltered existence where we were all the same—kids of professors and teachers. Then we went to the San Joaquin Valley in California and it was quite different. There was much more diversity and different values. In Iowa, you were appreciated for being smart. In California, you were admired for being pretty and being fashionable, and I was neither of those things.

Poverty and scarcity marked the development of more than one leader. Richard Bissen's story illustrated how the lack of material goods and a life of humble labor later translated into a value for appreciating and understanding of others.

> We had a taro patch, called a *loi* in Hawaiian, to earn some extra money and pay for my tuition. It was in a fishing village called Kahalua, where my mom had come from. My father and I spent a lot of our weekends tending that. I kind of resented it, but at the same time understood why. Later I worked in the canning factory, the lowest of the low. If you can't get any other job, you work there. I've done all kinds of work. But now when I look across at a jury, they are just like my family. I know how to talk to them. I don't know exactly how it happened, but I know how to get into someone else's skin.

One of the most remarkable stories about adversity was Leotis Watson's admission that he spent time on the streets of San Francisco—homeless, but not hopeless.

The turning point for everything was—homelessness. One morning I was sitting in this restaurant, sipping on this cup of chocolate all night long, because I had no place to go. I came out, it was foggy, and a thought hit me. "Leotis, you don't have to be here going about these changes. There are people who care about you. It matters not what you think of yourself. Matters not how low you think you are at this time. WAKE UP!" I said to God, "I know I have done some crazy things, but I am not a bad person. If you can see in your heart and give me mercy, I will change my life around." This was a life-changing moment.

Whether through a dramatic awakening, as in Leotis's case, or a more evolutionary process, clarity about what the leaders felt called to do emerged. It was often brought forth through an inner strength born of adversity and a need to "get clear" about what they wanted to do with their lives. It was prompted by opportunity.

CALLED BY OPPORTUNITY

On the flip side of adversity, opportunities focused on vocational callings. Not surprisingly, opportunities came knocking earlier and more often for male members of dominant cultures and more privileged classes than for females or individuals of minority status. Nevertheless, opportunities were either recognized and maximized by the former or created and built on by the latter. Gary Rasmussen expressed it best: "There are so many junctures and crossroads in one's life. It is kind of like going out on a limb of a tree. Each time, your choices get more and more refined." As each of the 36 leaders experienced opportunities and made decisions accordingly, they were brought closer to their life's calling. For the majority of males, multiple opportunities presented themselves, and they had the good sense and ability to make the most of them. Chet Bradley recounted numerous opportunities for stretching and growing as a leader.

> "I was given the opportunity to lead. People who are given some talent have to share it. In this part of Africa we are communalistic—we are supposed to be there for one another."
>
> —*Kuami Pianim*

I was named President of the freshman class of my high school. I don't remember what I did, but I was elected. I competed in all the sports and that probably had a bit to do with my leadership because I was captain of teams and played quarterback for football, which is a leadership role. People would give me the opportunity to go for something or I would see that something was available and then go for it on my own.

Ian Fox, a New Zealand principal, recounted similar opportunity that came his way as a young teacher.

Since I was usually one of the only males in my early teaching positions, I was given leadership roles. My principal always provided opportunities for me to do things and gave me freedom and responsibility to do it. I was allowed to develop areas of interest and then strength.

Michael Barber was aware that one opportunity led to another in his journey toward a life calling. Early in his teaching career, he became conscious of the role his principles played in workplace decision making, and this awareness helped him when he moved from being a teacher to being a paid employee of a teacher's union.

I learned a lot about standing my ground and not compromising my principles. The crunch point came toward the end of my time when the government introduced some national tests. We organized a boycott of the tests, and I represented the six unions in this country and led the negotiations about how to change them so that they would be better implemented.

While leadership opportunities might appear to have fallen into their laps, it has to be said that beyond the stereotype of privileged majority male leadership opportunity, leadership opportunity was offered because the individuals were judged to be capable of the task. Furthermore, not only were they recognized for qualities that would make them likely leadership candidates, but they also jumped on the opportunities that came their way.

Minorities and females often had to work harder to recognize and create their opportunities to step into leadership roles. For Leotis Watson, surviving homelessness provided motivation for finding and making opportunities for himself. He spoke at length of the transitional opportunities that finally allowed him to move forward.

After all of this time, I was still trying to find out who was Leotis? Not what I've done, but who I really am. For a while, I was doing odd jobs. I was motivated, trying to get back up. So I went to a 7–11 in Hempstead, a little town behind the times. They had built streets around hanging trees. I worked for a manager named Blackie. I walked in and said, "How are you doing? My name is Leotis" . . . and I start facing the products the front way, and I go in and clean the bathroom and finally Mr. Blackie says, "OK, you are good on the floor. Let's see how you work this register and make change and work with the customer." I had the cash register singing Yankee Doodle Came to Town. Customer service was like they had never seen before. I had everybody smiling and had everything in harmony. This was just my next step to success. I am moving good and I know my calling. He called me a wetback, but I know who I am and it runs right off. We built a good relationship because I knew who I was and what I wanted to do.

After taking a career break to raise her two children, Mandy Macleod, Headmistress of St. John's International School in Belgium, used her knowledge of special education to create a preprimary private school for 40 children. She later leveraged her school into a consolidation with St. John's to gain better opportunities for her students.

> I had two small children and once they were settled in school, I began to work part-time. It was quite frustrating for me because I didn't feel occupied intellectually. An opportunity arose to run a very small private school for the employees of 3M. . . . I was able to negotiate with St. John's to bring that school under their umbrella. That was really the beginning.

Similarly, Christine Rodriguez, a vice president at Rockwell Automation, needed 14 years to complete her bachelor's degree due to child-rearing responsibilities. Once at Rockwell, however, she finished her degree work and seized opportunities as they arose.

> I had my first child when I was 18. It took me awhile to get my education, but I was determined because of what I saw my parents build as a result of theirs. I took classes at night and on the weekends and eventually got a job with Rockwell as a clerk typist. They recognized my drive, ambition, and work ethic. I worked my way to the top of the administrative ranks, but decided that I wanted to go on in a communications career. I saw opportunities and took them, spending a lot of time learning on the job. My mentor committed to work with me as I broke out of the secretarial ranks and into the professional ranks as an editor of the employee newspaper. I went on to positions in media relations and executive relations. . . . I eventually became the director of the department where I had started as secretary.

Helen Clark articulated the general dilemma faced by women who pursue leadership opportunities. "As a woman, you have to be twice as good. It's very difficult to prove oneself."

Denese Henare, nevertheless, found that leadership opportunity was encouraged, almost bestowed, due to her family heritage.

> My family tradition is one of working within the system. My grandfather was a member of Parliament. My uncle was a colonel in the army and a revered and respected leader. So there is a legacy to carry—I've always understood that sense of service. I have been purposed, I have been truly purposed.

Opportunities bestowed or created helped the 36 leaders find ways in which they could live out their values through work experience. Early work experiences, in turn, began to further define the difference between a job and a life calling. Their work responsibilities became the means by which refined vocational calling would be accomplished.

CALLED BY EARLY WORK EXPERIENCE

For most of us, early work experiences help to pay the bills while we continue to conduct a search for the right vocational match to our interests and skills. For the 36 leaders, such searching helped them to experiment with jobs that more clearly aligned with their developing calling. That is, they searched for the type of work that would allow them to live out their values while pursuing personal goals for making the world a better place. As Mechai Viraviadya put it, "Why work in a job where you can't change anything?"

> "I worked in corporate law, but it didn't satisfy my soul."
>
> —*Denese Henare*

As a young journalist, Mechai learned the value of the work, but also learned that his mission was to act on life, not report on it.

> I learned from the gutter, not the university. To me the world is not a writing or talking world, but a doing world. When you do it, you change people far more easily than writing about it. As a journalist, I wrote about it, talked about it on radio and television. Everyone said it was great, then they forgot about it. But when I realized that and got a few to start doing it, that makes the difference.

Early career experimentation helped define a calling by clarifying what the young leaders wanted to do with their lives and how they might go about it. Michael Barber described such experience in struggling to understand and deal with "the system."

> Before I went to college, I cared for four seriously brain-damaged boys. I kept running into conflict with the hierarchy. I thought they were hide-bound. I wasn't critical of the care of the education that the students got, but the number of people in my situation passing though. I was quite rebellious and difficult about it. There was a restlessness about that and the recognition of learning to deal with hierarchies of a different sort than I was used to. Challenging tradition but not rejecting it. I drew on that experience a lot when I worked at the university.

Julianne Lowe's early career journey ran an interesting and diverse gamut of enlightening experiences.

> I went to Australia when I was 19. I did everything there. I was waitressing, bartending, and even worked in a brothel without realizing it. I got sacked pretty quickly, mind you. I've had lots and lots of jobs . . . experimenting and gaining heaps of experience. Got fired a few times for not playing hanky panky. I went back to Rotorua [New Zealand] . . . to an intensive course in audiology. I loved it. When I came back, I was asked to set up and run the audiology unit single-handed. I was only about 22 or 23. Because of my

nursing skills and my experience in the shop, I was good with old people and listened to them and could deal with the emotional issues. It's one thing to know the technical skills, but if you can't understand them as people, you really can't help them. That's what I wanted to do, help people.

Early work experience gave Rich Teerlink an opportunity to try on the values learned from his parents.

I went to work in public accounting. I have always had a great interest in the success of organizations and success of everybody in the organization, not just those at the top. This goes back to the influence of my dad and my mother. She said there is one rule to follow, the golden rule. That means everyone has [a] say.

Beth Stevenson also observed that her path to her vocational calling was not immediately clear.

At one time I had to draw [a picture of] my journey. I looked like a Yo-Yo, where I was bouncing back and forth between kids and health. I started out knowing that I wanted to be doing something related to education as a process. I ran day camps and taught. Eventually, I worked in developmental psychology and volunteered in health. Went back to school and got a public health degree, but that was work in hospitals focusing on education and not with kids. Meanwhile, I was doing a lot of volunteer work with the American Cancer Society, fundraising, and community organizing. So when this job came up, it allowed me to be able to look at things holistically, people holistically. The education model works best when we are able to look at kids as a whole.

Brenda Schoonover spent time in the Philippines developing a deep respect and understanding for cultural values and service dependent on the needs of others as opposed to what she might have presumed their needs to be.

I was a member of the charter group of the first Peace Corps volunteers. I learned that almost every culture has the same set of values, but it is the order in which they place the values that can cause confusion and misunderstanding.

Working as a young teacher, Ian Fox discovered the satisfaction of accomplishment found when he could see children learning and gaining from the influence he had on them.

I remember the name Malcolm Polite—it's a name I'll never forget because he was the first 5-year-old who I knew could read, and read well, and I knew that I was responsible for that! It was thrilling because he was the first boy I had who couldn't do anything when he started, and he was really quite confident at the end.

As a young man, Ulice Payne was fortunate to work as a business intern for both U.S. Steel and IBM. He recounts the impact this had on his future career path.

> Those jobs taught me about business and commerce from leaders in their environments. I learned a lot about how they went about their business, how they hired people, how they are part of the communities and the pride they had in their work. The chance to get exposed to these world leaders as a young student was remarkable. I learned a lot at a critical stage of my life. Their whole thing was "We are U.S. Steel. We are IBM. We don't follow others; we set the stage." It was very important to me in forming my thoughts about leadership.

As their stories unfolded, then, the 36 leaders shared a collective tale of being called to their ultimate leadership purpose. It was, notably, a search for calling influenced more often by early work experience than by chance discovery.

Lessons Learned

The stories shared in this chapter begin to frame the experience of 36 leaders who were formed, not born. Within that portrayal, leadership was not a primary goal for any of the interviewed leaders. Rather, through childhood and young adult experiences, the journey to leadership evolved toward a life calling—a calling undergirded by core values.

It is through description of early formation experience that the foundation of a coherent leadership model emerges. It is a foundation, moreover, that promotes understanding of the very roots of leadership. We begin to observe the genesis of leadership, that is, how an internal coherence about leadership purpose is centered and nurtured.

This is particularly important because, while there is considerable research about leadership development in leadership contexts (e.g., Day, 2000; McCauley, 2001), there is much less attention to what shapes and calls individuals to such contexts. This deficiency is undoubtedly due in part to the fact that leadership development and personal development are difficult to separate and share many of the same dynamics (McCauley, Moxley, & Van Velsor, 1998). Insight as to what brings individuals to the leadership gate is, nevertheless, of great interest and value to practitioners and scholars alike.

In this investigation, 36 leaders identified influences that reinforced core values and prompted exploration of vocational calling. They specifically described

- How core leadership values were *shaped* by family and community, cultural context, and mentor influence
- How they were *called* to leadership through adversity, opportunity, and early work experience

LESSONS ABOUT THE SHAPING OF LEADERS

In sharing perceptions about their formation, the 36 leaders revealed that their core values were strongly shaped by family and community, cultural context, and mentor influence.

Three primary lessons surface regarding the shaping of leadership core values. First, it would seem that *it takes a village to raise a leader.* Immediate and extended family and friends lent important hands to the shaping of a foundational value base. Second, *cultural context provides a powerful milieu for value formation.* Both subtly and overtly, the cultural context of the young leader models and molds the young leader. Last, *influential mentors come in all shapes and sizes.* Mentors, whether singly or as groups, guide young minds, demonstrate values in action, and reinforce values already established.

> "I credit my parents a lot. They gave me a great upbringing. . . . They made sacrifices for me. I don't want to shed a poor light on my family. I think that is true of everyone from Hawaii . . . so I push myself as hard as I can."
>
> — *Richard Bissen*

Ultimately, the leaders' core values were born from the interaction of people, places, and events experienced in youth. Both in childhood and as young adults, they took advantage of positive role models, contexts, and experiences to build a personal set of values. Notably, those who had negative experiences seemed to be able to transform the lesson learned into a value of opposite quality.

The values most frequently advocated across 36 interviews were

1. Human dignity, equality, and diversity
2. Hard work and perseverance
3. High standards of responsibility in self and others
4. Competence, skill, and knowledge
5. Productive thinking habits (e.g., analytic, creative)
6. Service to others
7. Making a difference in the world

Oriented by such values, the leaders proceeded to explore the compelling life callings that would eventually define their leadership commitment and purpose.

LESSONS ABOUT LIFE'S CALLING

In exploring their life's calling, the 36 leaders took advantage of three approaches that helped them to discover the right match for their value orientation. First, *they used adversity to sharpen their vision for how they wanted to invest their lives.* By living through tough times, each of the leaders forged inner strength and conviction about what he or she wanted to contribute to the world. Second, *they seized and created leadership opportunities.* Such opportunities helped them explore

> "Over time I looked around and found that everyone is following."
>
> — *Ulice Payne*

leadership callings aligned to their values and interests. Last, *they used early work experiences to refine and clarify their leadership purpose.* Such experience was an important practical element in moving the leaders toward their ultimate leadership roles.

The combination of strength and conviction that arose from early adversity and leadership opportunity and experience helped the leaders define their life's calling. Experience, both positive and negative, broadened their horizons, as did their knowledge and skill. They learned what questions to ask of themselves and others. Most important, they began to form criteria for aligning their work to their values.

A LESSON WITHIN THE LESSONS

The formation paths followed by these 36 leaders led to life experiences in which core values were ultimately in alignment with vocational callings. Life, of course, isn't linear, and neither was any leader's journey to his or her leadership destination. Nevertheless, all the leaders described having benefited from repeated opportunities for

- Building and testing their values through interactions with their environment and significant others
- Defining and articulating their life's calling by making the most of challenges, experimenting with work, and finding opportunities to spread their wings

One lesson to be observed, then, is that core leadership values are initially shaped by family and community, cultural context, and mentor influences. The other lesson is that the call to a leadership vocation both arises from, and further shapes, core values through adversity, opportunity, and work experience. The lesson within these two lessons is that there is a dynamic relationship between the shaping of values and a call to leadership. Values form the base from which a vocational search is launched. Vocational exploration, in turn, is a means to refine and reinforce core values. A picture thereby emerges of a progressive and dynamic leadership formation, a formation that interactively moves from value formation to vocational calling (see Figure 2.1).

In Chapter 3, we will observe how this formation further evolves as leaders prepare for and accept the mantle of leadership within chosen fields.

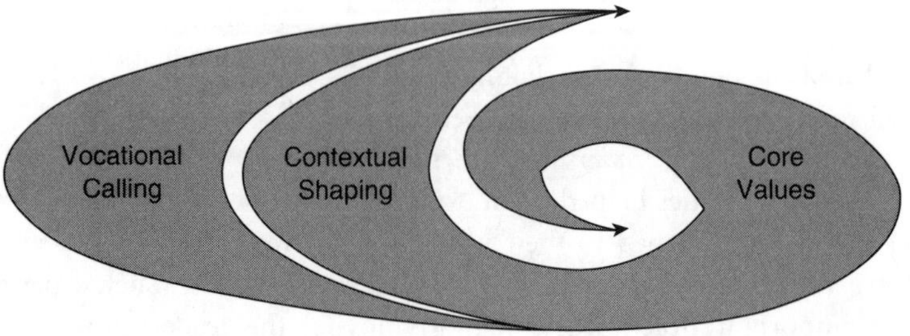

A. Core values shaped by the contextual influence of family, community, culture, and mentors form a base from which exploration of vocational calling is launched.

B. Vocational calling emerges from adversity, opportunity, and early work experience to both actualize and reinforce core values.

Figure 2.1   A Leadership Formation Dynamic: Values Shaped by Context and Calling

Further Conversation

You are again invited to actively join in this unfolding leadership conversation. The discussion points here, given the preceding chapter content, address how you have been shaped and called to your leadership experience. Your participation in the conversation will be facilitated by Further Conversation Exercises 2.1 and 2.2 (both of which can be done either individually or in the company of colleagues per your preference and opportunity).

EXERCISE 2.1   Further Conversation: The Shaping of Core Values

A. What are the core values that orient your approach to life and leadership?

B. How did you form those core values (i.e., where did they come from)?

EXERCISE 2.2   Further Conversation: The Calling

A. When and how did you first become aware of your vocational interests?

B. How was your vocational calling influenced by adversity, opportunity, or early work experience?

3

Commitment

As an acorn takes root, or a field flourishes in the Spring, they grew in their commitments bit by bit.

—Daloz, Keen, Keen, and Parks (1997, p. 196)

Committed

There is a difference between deciding and making a commitment to one's vocational calling. As a pilot friend once observed, you might rather easily discover an interest in flying an airplane. It is taking off on a solo flight for the first time, however, that turns a decision to fly into a commitment to fly and land a plane safely.

So it was with the commitment of exemplary leaders. They didn't just decide one day to devote their selves to a particular purpose. Something happened that turned initial interests into life-defining commitments. From core values and an aligned sense of calling, they grew into a deeper emotional and intellectual embrace of purpose and associated action. Such commitment was spurred by an evolving belief that they could have a meaningful impact on what they valued most in life. It was commitment that was nurtured, first and foremost, by a growing sense of self-efficacy.

Self-efficacy is a concept offered by social cognition theorists to explain the perceptions we hold about our ability to perform a given task and effect resulting consequences (Bandura, 1997). A sense of self-efficacy either empowers one to take on a challenge or limits one's ability to do so. Afflicted with a low sense of self-efficacy, you are inclined to either not try or give up easily when confronted with a challenging task. Indeed, you might surmise that effort will be somehow lacking and results limited. Imbued with a high sense of self-efficacy, on the other hand, you are more eager to accept and act on challenging assignments. You would feel capable of handling the task and simultaneously anticipate a positive result.

Notably, the 36 interviewed leaders all conveyed a strong positive sense of self-efficacy. They were confident about their leadership capacity for favorably influencing the achievement of important results. They were also aware that such confidence grew from support and experience as they initially sought to achieve results and realize an impact within their chosen vocational callings.

COMMITTED THROUGH CONFIDENCE

The interviewed leaders were nudged toward leadership commitments by the reinforcing encouragement and feedback they received from valued mentors and advisors. Such feedback reached back to early childhood and continued to progress as the journey to leadership evolved.

> "I initially didn't start as a leader, but as part of a team. Often I would come up with an idea that was a little different and they would let me lead. Success built upon success."
>
> —CJ Nickerson

Beth Stevenson spoke of the effect her mother's words had on her feeling of empowerment as a child and later as an adult.

My mother would tell me very explicitly how I needed to look at myself to change the situation. I remember being in sixth grade and crying that I had no friends. My mother's response was, "What are you doing about it, what could you change?" It made me feel as though I had power over the situation. Today, I never lose sight of what I am trying to accomplish. I try to be centered, because there are always so many distractions. Creating a good process is critical in order to allow for ambiguity but keep the focus so that things keep moving. I work hard on figuring out what tools are necessary to work through the process.

For other leaders, confidence-building reinforcement came from the workplace. Mandy Macleod recalled a superintendent who showed faith in her and the reinforcing results that occurred.

She offered me the job of principal for one year with the option to go back into the classroom. I got great satisfaction from seeing the progression of the students and the satisfaction of the parents.

Jeanne Dukes credited an early mentor with turning her self-confidence around. Jeanne had experienced a dominating father whose word was the law. It took her years of trial and error to start to believe in her own voice.

My boss got me involved in state politics . . . to argue for what's in the best interests of these kids. He encouraged me to go back to school and he sponsored me in an administrator [preparation] program.

Such opportunities to experience leadership with reinforcing feedback about efforts fostered growth. Many of the interviewed leaders experienced supervisors who took time to talk to them about leadership. Such counsel not only helped the novice leaders formulate their life goals, but also helped them to begin to understand the impact they might be able to realize. CJ Nickerson shared one such simple, but important, encounter in his life—one that caused him to begin to think more for himself. "One of my professors in my master's program kept telling me, 'This is okay for a textbook answer, but I want to know what you think.'"

COMMITTED THROUGH CONSEQUENCE

Advice and feedback from respected sources nurtured the leaders' expectations for success in their chosen field. They were also motivated by early tastes of the satisfaction that comes from impacting a calling of value to them. Ross Gilbert recalled an experience he had in college that brought an awareness of the result of his efforts.

> "It's not just about words, or espoused values, it's about action and results."
>
> —Boon Yoon Chiang

> When I was at teachers' college, I used to go to youth camp and I'd be the one directing the circuit games, a very complex organization. I'd be the one they'd put in charge of that sort of activity. I wanted to make sure that things were done right. It was important to me that everyone remained active. It gave me satisfaction to see that this happened.

CJ Nickerson spoke of similar satisfaction that he received from seeing the impact of his work.

> I really get a charge out of getting the job done. When I can conceptualize a way to meet a need that was important to make things better for people, I'm happy.

An early experience sewed the seeds of confidence in Ulice Payne, paving the way for later confidence as a leader.

> I was asked to be on a televised Junior High quiz program. Our team went to the finals four times. That was big. You had to be expert in something and your team counted on you I felt responsibility for my school, my teachers, and my town. There was a sense of leading the train and showing that this little steel town can be good.

The development of self-efficacy as a leader was a longer road to hoe for many of the women interviewed. Helen Clark and Nola Hambleton indicated the need to be "twice as good" as a man to be taken seriously in their field of calling. Margo Dévai, head of a health education agency in Hungary, mentioned, somewhat bitterly, that it took her 25 years to be recognized for her worth. Even though she developed a strong self-concept from her family, she turned down leadership roles, never saw herself as a leader, and never had a female role model for how to balance leadership with family. Eventually, though, she recognized her own self-worth, as did others.

> There was no doubt that what I did was good. I was involved in different institutes, universities, and conferences and my colleagues saw it. . . . Finally, I was confident in my work. Then . . . I started to honor myself.

Similarly, Christine Rodriguez had to build her self-confidence over time. As a woman and person of color, she learned that she had to market herself and bring to light her skills and attributes.

> I can't tell you how many meetings there were where I would sit there and was afraid that what would come out of my mouth would be considered dumb or uninformed. Often I was thinking what the next person verbalized. As I gained confidence, I learned that my opinions counted and that I could add value to whatever was going on.

Whether through reinforcement from others or from the experience of a job well done, the 36 leaders were emotionally and intellectually turned on early and often by the effect—and potential—of their influence. Sooner for some, but eventually for all, a transforming perception of "self as leader" began to transpire. They began to recognize an alignment between their values and calling and the consequences of their behavior. Such awareness fueled conscious commitment to making a difference in their vocational field. Most important, it opened their minds to assuming leadership roles as the means to manifest core values within vocational callings.

Compelled

Having described a formative experience that progressed from the shaping of core values to reinforcing callings and deepening commitments, the leadership formation story now addresses why and how the mantle of leadership was assumed. Again, the leaders' interview reflections to this point suggest that none set out to become a leader. They did describe early interest in the fields that they were passionate about, whether it was education, law, medicine, science, government, journalism, art, or some other worthy endeavor. They wanted to make a difference, to improve the world and serve others, to be the best teacher, violinist, or other form of contributing citizen they could be. For all of that, however, they did not initially see themselves as leaders.

Interestingly, as the 36 reflections about leadership formation unfolded, early markers of leadership disposition were revealed. And, inevitably, commitments were made and roles assumed as the leaders sought to achieve goals aligned to core values. In other words, the 36 leaders were compelled to assume leadership roles. They were driven to such roles as the means to actualize their values and manifest their commitments.

COMPELLED BY PREDISPOSITION

If you are a leader, you probably identify with the predisposition to "figure it out." Many of the interviewed leaders recalled early experiences with the ability to "see" how things should go or come up with unique ideas. In addition to seeing things that were not so obvious to others, they described incidences of their ability to influence others and direct events early in life. Rod Chamberlain noted demonstrations of such proclivity in his childhood.

> "I always could see things that seemed self-evident to me, but not to others."
>
> —*Jeanne Dukes*

> I came from a church tradition where cards weren't allowed but ROOK was because it wasn't associated with gambling. In all the games we held a debriefing . . . how did someone win and what was the strategy. To this day it drives my wife crazy. . . . She says, "Just play the game. You don't have to dissect it." But it is built into me after all these years. . . . I'm constantly thinking about how things could work better.

CJ Nickerson described his ability to "see it" and the effect such insight had on his colleagues.

> I could conceptualize a way to meet a need that I thought was important to make things better for people. Early in my professional days others wouldn't see it, but they trusted me and so would go along with it. They would say, "We really didn't get it, but we know you got it and so we were willing to go along." I didn't see myself as a leader, but really part of a team. They knew that I would work hard and that my word was my bond. That led to acceptance.

In addition to the ability to figure it out, many of the leaders cited an early need to voice their opinions and stretch their sphere of influence. Helen Clark, while instilled with sound beliefs from her family, found that even at an early age she was able to argue her liberal viewpoint with her conservative father about how those beliefs should be lived out in practice. "I have always had a clear sense of what was right and wrong and what was fair and just."

Rich Teerlink talked about his early leadership effect on friends. Like Helen, he recognized his tendency to know his mind and let others know it as well.

> In high school, I was head of a HI-Y club. I was elected to be the president. I really don't know why; they must have seen something in me. When I was growing up, people would joke about Teerlink's rules. I wasn't bashful about saying this is right and this is wrong.

Both Julianne Lowe and Beth Stevenson felt dissatisfied within their family structures if they weren't taking some sort of leadership role when they felt the need presented itself. "When I see the need for an improvement to make, I voice it. I just found myself figuring out what we should do [and] then taking charge."

Beth surmised that birth order might have been a factor affecting her early disposition toward the exercise of leadership behavior.

> I was an oldest child, so I am always the person who is most comfortable making decisions or throwing out the first idea. Later in college I was drawn to personal service that required judgment. I would think about how to frame the activity to make sure it was good for everybody. I was good at troubleshooting.

Curiosity and collaboration were additional leadership qualities that were evident within many of the leaders at an early age. Denese Henare noted such qualities in her personal experience.

> I was always a curious child, very inquisitive. In school I was the consensus finder, looking for win/win. I learned from the Maori style of debate, which could go on all day and all night until everyone is heard and all views are tested.

Patrick Sayne shared his early and lasting understanding of the relationship between management and leadership as he reflected on his own ability to envision an idea and see it to fruition.

> A leader, in the inception, thinks [he or she] has a better idea and wants to get it going . . . but someone [also] has to organize. My former wife used to say that if I saw a basket of puppies, I would want to sort and categorize them. Who knows what causes that. I think you can make a pretty good manager with no desire to be a leader, but I don't think you can make a leader out of someone who ultimately doesn't want to be one. I think a manager is someone who provides organization and direction, but a leader provides a vision.

Though the leaders didn't initially aspire to leadership, they described early capacity for it. Such capacity was often informally exercised during their youth. It was capacity lying in wait for circumstances to necessitate its full maturation.

COMPELLED BY NEED AND OPPORTUNITY

Given early evidence of leadership tendencies, the 36 leaders nevertheless maintained a youthful ambivalence about formal leadership roles. There was need for additional motivation, some culminating pressure that would propel them beyond a vocational commitment to a leadership commitment within that vocation. As it happened, such motivation commonly arose from encounters with barriers within systems, barriers that were blocking the fulfillment of the leaders' vocational callings.

> "I always rejected being a bureaucrat. I went over to the CEU as director of the newly established human rights program. There was no human rights education effort before this program."
>
> — Gabor Halmai

Frustration with a system as it existed—either its structure or policies or both—was what most frequently pushed the interviewed leaders forward to leadership. Their recognition of a leadership void or ineffective leadership behavior is what most often precipitated their stepping up to leadership responsibilities.

Bucking a system that was perceived to be unfair characterized the coming of age of some leaders. Early in his career, Michael Barber supported a boycott of state testing, organized by the union he worked for, because he perceived the implementation of the test as very poor. From that entry to leadership, he promoted change and improvement through writing and academia, which led to a position of influence within Tony Blair's Labor Party.

> When Labor won after all of those years, there was lots to learn from watching the previous performance . . . what was good, what was bad, how to do it. We applied that in a new philosophy of implementation.

Helen Clark took a more deliberate reform path, working in politics 25 years before reaching the pinnacle of her country's leadership as prime minister. The daughter of a Conservative Nationalist, Helen became a left-wing activist in order to promote her perception of a better system based on the core values of fairness, opportunity, and security. "I want to build a society where everyone has the opportunity to fulfill their talents . . . and has access to quality education to do so."

Ian Fox was mindful of his Presbyterian grandfather's admonition that a job worth doing is a job worth doing well. He also loved the challenge and excitement of meaningful work done well. In his early teaching career, he found that he had to step up to leadership positions to insure that decisions were student centered. He couldn't resist the opportunity to take the lead when it led to decisions that were better for his students.

There was an advisor who'd come around to small schools to suggest certain things, like timetables. I could never find one that suited me. In the end, I had to develop my own. I always had to be assured that the students were getting the best opportunities that I could possibly provide. I wasn't prepared to compromise for the sake of expedience.

A leadership vacuum can be a blessing or a curse. For the 36 leaders, such voids were often opportunities. Rod Chamberlain described his unanticipated opportunity to step into the breech.

I was fortunate or unfortunate enough to end up in a situation where there was a lack of leadership. I was a [K–12] teacher and wanted to be a college teacher. . . . When I told my academic dean that I was looking at a college position, he offered me the role of curriculum director. I was totally surprised.

Many of the interviewed leaders spoke of the motivation to assume leadership roles coming from a perception that they could do it as well or better than the next person could. In his career as a prosecutor, Richard Bissen didn't go after leadership roles unless he felt better prepared to assume such roles than others.

I usually find that if I am okay with the current leadership, I don't take part or I will help out. But if I get to a certain position in an organization and think I can do it as well as the rest of the people on the list, then I will get involved. I find that pattern in myself. I will go in if I feel that I would regret it if I didn't. When my current position became available, I didn't want to apply until I heard the names of others who were applying.

Observing the mistakes of other leaders encouraged Bob Knight, CFO of Paul Homes, to consider leadership prospects for himself.

I saw a lot of companies fail because they had leaders with unusual personalities. I watched those leaders fail to get respect because their actions spoke so loud that you couldn't hear their words.

Frank Lukasavitz, cofounder of the Milwaukee Institute of Art and Design, embraced a leadership role out of rebellion against a failing art school that he felt was misdirected in its mission and management.

We were sitting round and someone said, "Let's start a new school." Someone else said, "You can't just start a school," and I said, "Why not?" We shook hands and each kicked in 100 bucks. I was head of the committee to find a facility and seek accreditation. We begged and borrowed and built stuff and soon started the school with 32 students . . . all in the same year.

The 36 leaders all acknowledged a need or opportunity that compelled them to say yes to leadership. Kuami Pianim, CEO of New World Investments Ltd in Ghana, observed that this might be a bit serendipitous.

> I think sometimes leadership just drops on people. You happen to be the person in the right place at a historically defining moment, and then you either take up the mantle or you do not.

The 36 interview reflections suggest, however, that leadership opportunity was more than happenstance. Such opportunity was more likely to be seized by those who were committed to a purpose and, thereby, compelled to assume leadership responsibilities.

Lessons Learned

The reflections of 36 exemplary leaders described a formation path that progressed beyond values and calling to leadership commitment. Notably, the leaders' movement down that path was energized toward progressive self-efficacy by inner coherence about compelling purpose.

> "I just wanted to be the best violinist I could become."
>
> —Don Hazelwood

LESSONS ABOUT BECOMING COMMITTED TO LEAD

Through growing awareness that they could exercise a positive impact on goals aligned to their core values, the 36 leaders experienced a seductive pull toward leadership commitments. They became more deeply committed as their *confidence in their ability* to have an impact within their sphere of influence was reinforced by positive feedback from others. The opportunity to test themselves in informal leadership roles nurtured their commitment within their vocational purpose. Observing the *positive consequence of actions* was also a powerful source of reinforcement.

> "I was chosen for this path, I didn't choose it."
>
> —Richard Bissen

LESSONS ABOUT BEING COMPELLED TO LEAD

Making a commitment to more formal and prominent leadership roles was ultimately compelled by the leaders' predispositions, as well as the needs and opportunities they encountered within vocational callings. The leaders

"I've always been a go-getter. I am a bit of a perfectionist I think. As I grew up, through school, everything I went for, I wanted to be the best. I remember very early in my junior year in high school, I joined an extracurricular club which had very senior people, and I became president of the club!"

—*Alex Banful*

observed an early and *compelling predisposition toward curiosity, creativity, and collaboration* and to "figure it out" when confronted by problems and tasks. Those precursors of leadership potential were often recognized and encouraged by mentors along the formation path. The leaders also felt *compelled to step up and lead when a leadership need or opportunity was apparent.* Leadership vacuums that imperiled organizational success often precipitated their transition to leadership roles.

A LESSON WITHIN THE LESSONS

It was inevitable, for these 36 exemplary leaders, that saying no to leadership was not an option. As they moved down their formation path, they became deeply committed to vocational callings that were rooted in core values, and they were subsequently compelled to assume leadership roles that were aligned with these values. If they wanted to achieve the goals related to their callings, they would have to accept the mantle of leadership.

This description further defines the foundation of a coherent leadership model (see Figure 3.1). That foundation (as initially described in Chapter 2) originates with the shaping of core values and the exploration of vocational calling. It is then expanded and reinforced (as described in this chapter) by commitment to meaningful service within a calling, including the acceptance of leadership roles. This genesis flows from core values that center internal coherence about leadership purpose. Values are initially shaped by context and then progressively reinforced as the individual is called, committed, and compelled to lead. Thus, a dynamic model of coherent leadership continues to unfold. At this point, the evolving model describes the coherency, that is, a logical and consistent relationship of parts, within leadership formation. Chapters 4 through 7 will examine how that coherency is extended through congruent leadership performance.

Further Conversation

This conversation invites your active reflection, at this juncture, to address when, why, and how you resolved leadership commitments along your leadership formation path. The following exercise (which can be done either individually or in the company of colleagues) will facilitate that reflection.

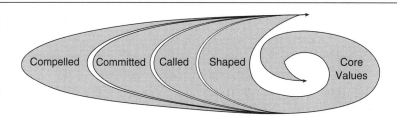

A. Core values shaped by the contextual influence of family, community, culture, and mentors form a base from which exploration of vocational calling is launched.

B. Vocational calling emerges from adversity, opportunity, and early work experience to both actualize and reinforce core values

C. Vocational commitment cultivates leadership knowledge, skill, and disposition, and further actualizes and reinforces core values.

D. Context and circumstance compels the assumption of a leadership role that fully actualizes core values.

Figure 3.1   A Leadership Formation Dynamic: Core Values are Formed and Actualized

EXERCISE 3.1 Further Conversation: Leadership Commitment

A. At what point did your career choice rise to a vocational commitment?

B. What precipitated that shift?

C. When and in what fashion did you develop an awareness of your ability to favorably influence the achievement of goals?

D. How did you come to assume a leadership role in your chosen field?

E. Why did you find it necessary or desirable to assume that role?

Part II

Leadership Performed

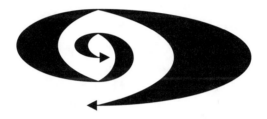

What you are speaks so loudly that I cannot hear what you say.

—Emerson (1911)

The stories shared in Part I of this narrative described how 36 leaders were formed. Early life experiences shaped values and commitments that, in turn, compelled the acceptance of leadership roles. The narrative continues in Part II, with description of how leadership performance emerges from formative experience. The interviewed leaders observe a congruent alignment between their espoused values and subsequent character and behavior. They also portray prominent leadership performance connections to the social, emotional, and reflective nature of human capacity.

4

Value Aligned

Integrity knows the interdependence of things.

—Daft and Lengel (1998, p. 174)

The Performance Story

This chapter introduces a story of extended leadership coherence—an account of interconnected harmony among what 36 leaders professed to value, be, and do. It is a story that unfolds across the following chapters to capture how, in the minds of the interviewed leaders, leadership performance was markedly aligned to values and purpose, both in character and behavior (see Figure 4.1).

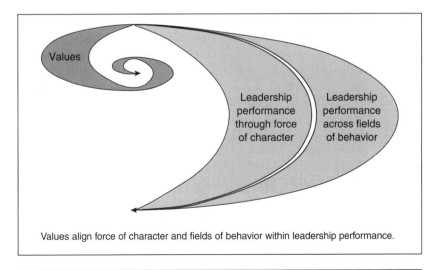

Values align force of character and fields of behavior within leadership performance.

Figure 4.1   Alignment of Leadership Values, Character, and Behavior Within Performance

In the larger picture, this account about aligned values, character, and behavior begins to define the essence of how 36 leaders conducted the leadership business of influencing others toward the achievement of their goals. That is, the storytellers reveal how values gave rise to the force of character and fields of behavior that connected leadership to human capacity for growth and achievement.

Performed as Formed

With conscious perspective of how they were formed, so were these 36 leaders disposed to perform. As described in Chapters 2 and 3, early life experiences formed the values and commitments that eventually compelled these individuals to assume leadership responsibilities. The trail continues from there as core values and compelling purpose are strongly referenced in the leaders' perceptions of how they executed their leadership roles. Indeed, their reflections about leadership performance reveal that the more internally coherent they became about the alignment of values and purpose, the more certain they became about *how* to lead in a compatible manner. Internal coherence about values and purpose, in effect, was extended to congruent leadership character and behavior. As Richard Teerlink put it, "How we behave begins with values."

For example, Mechai Viraviadya was passionate about his value for the dignity of all human life and the eradication of poverty in Thailand. Consequently, his self-described performance as President of the Population Development Association was characteristically respectful and fair toward those he worked with. His aligned behavior provided egalitarian structures to assure everyone had a voice and opportunity to contribute. Similarly, Kuami Pianim described how his actions were aligned to his appreciation for the wisdom of others. Through his extensive travels throughout Ghana as a young man, he had concluded that "these illiterate people are far smarter than most of us. If you can articulate a problem in a way that they understand, they will give you the solution." Subsequently, Kuami's leadership performance was oriented by his belief in the capacity of others whenever he acted to empower the people he felt privileged to lead.

Embedded in Character

Chapter 2 described seven prominent values that were observed across the leadership formation experiences of 36 leaders. These included

1. Human dignity, equality, and diversity

2. Hard work and perseverance

3. High standards of responsibility for self and others

4. Competence in skill and knowledge

5. Productive thinking habits (e.g., analytic, creative)

6. Service to others

7. Making a difference in the world

It was with frequent reference to their value orientations that the interviewees shared their sense of self as leaders, that is, their personal leadership character. They professed that leadership performance was necessarily in character with fundamental values forged during leadership formation. Such value alignment behind the force of leadership character will be further examined in Chapter 5—an examination highlighted by the leaders' humble, passionate, and contemplative characterization of their leadership performance.

Acted Out in Behavior

Having observed that their leadership performance was first and foremost aligned in character to core values, the further reflections of 36 leaders reveal that what was valued in mind and character was acted out in behavior. Chapter 6 examines such extended alignment of values and character to action across three prominent fields of leadership behavior (i.e., community building, centering, and thinking) as described by the leaders.

Connected to Capacity

Observations from the field about value-aligned leadership character and behavior are of considerable interest and value within themselves. Such revelation becomes even more meaningful for the insight it offers about how leaders influence others to achieve their goals in real-life contexts.

The interviewed leaders did not separate what they did from who they were and what they believed. How they behaved was part and parcel of who they were, and who they were had everything to do with values forged during their leadership formation. There is further interpretation, however, within the leaders' perceptions of leadership performance—how they conducted themselves toward the fulfillment of purpose.

The thematic patterns that emerged from the shared stories of 36 leaders about aligned values, character, and behavior collectively reveal the essential nature of their leadership influence on others toward the achievement of goals. That is, they exercise force of character across fields of behavior in a manner that connected their leadership to human capacity for growth and achievement. It matters not whether such attention was intuitive or conscious or a combination of both. What becomes apparent within the reflections shared in Chapter 7 is that the leaders' approach to performance was dominated by connections to others, connections that were prominently social, emotional, and reflective in nature.

Lessons Learned

For anyone who has experienced the services of a chiropractor, the concept of alignment is familiar. Chiropractors make it their business to align the body from head to toe. Every person who has suffered back, shoulder, or neck pain understands the effect of a misaligned spine. When the core skeletal system is out of whack, attention to other matters is distracted, effectiveness tumbles, and health care costs increase.

In their interview responses about leadership performance, the 36 leaders described attributes of character and behavior strongly aligned to their sense of self and value-driven purpose. They collectively described a path that progressed from the formation of core values to congruent character and behavior. There is also a reciprocal relationship to be observed within this alignment of values, character, and behavior—a two-way street you might say. An inner coherency about values is naturally extended to encompass performance through congruent character and behavior. Congruent character and behavior, in turn, reinforce core values (see Figure 4.2).

How important is the alignment of leadership values, character, and behavior? At this point in their storytelling, the 36 leaders reveal their perception of a key to leadership success. They describe the importance of congruency between character and behavior and internal coherency between values and purpose. Such congruency aligned goals that merited leadership attention with force of character and how one behaved as a leader.

Ultimately, it is from such description of value-aligned character and behavior that we begin to glean a deeper understanding about how leaders establish productive connections (e.g., social, emotional, reflective) to those they aspire to influence.

Further Conversation

It is time for you to rejoin this leadership conversation. The conversation at this point invites an initial reflection about the importance of aligned values,

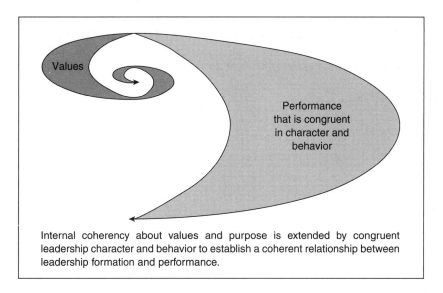

Internal coherency about values and purpose is extended by congruent leadership character and behavior to establish a coherent relationship between leadership formation and performance.

Figure 4.2   The Extension of Coherent Leadership by Congruent Leadership Performance

character, and behavior to your leadership performance. Your participation in the conversation will be facilitated by the following Further Conversation exercise (again, to be conducted either individually or in the company of colleagues, as you prefer).

EXERCISE 4.1   Further Conversation: The Value of Value Alignment

With reference to your prior reflection in Further Conversation Exercise 2.1:

A.   What are the core values that orient your general approach to life?

B.   What are the core values that orient your approach to leadership?

C.   How are you aware of your core values in the conduct of your day-to-day life?

D.   How are you aware of your core values in the conduct of your leadership role?

E.   How would your leadership be affected if it were "valueless"?

5

In Character

Leader traits contribute significantly to the prediction of leader effectiveness, leader emergence, and leader advancement.

—Zaccaro, Kemp, and Bader (2004, p. 119)

Performance Through Force of Character

The 36 interviewed leaders were "real characters." They were real leaders in diverse leadership roles across a wide range of contexts. Their uniqueness of character and accomplishment was such that they stood out and were noticed. Moreover, the interviewees were very self-aware of their defining character traits.

Character is the peculiar quality, or sum of qualities, by which a person is distinguished from others; it is the unique stamp imprinted by the interaction of nature, education, or habit describing who that person really is. It is a term used to describe a person's attributes, traits, or abilities. Character is also associated with the moral or ethical principles that motivate and direct one's life.

It is notable, then, that when asked to describe their leadership performance, that is, their defining approaches to influencing others toward the achievement of goals, the 36 leaders most often spoke about the importance of character first. Furthermore, their reflections strongly suggested that their leadership performance was necessarily in character because it naturally emanated from their core values (e.g., human dignity, hard work, high standards, competence, productive thinking, service to others, and making a difference).

In describing attributes of their leadership character, the interviewed leaders shared the essence of *who* they perceived themselves to be. For example, Richard Bissen perceived himself as trustworthy, and Beth Stevenson described herself as empathetic. Such self-described character traits address an important dimension of leadership performance. In the minds of the interviewed leaders, the way they saw themselves, as well as the way they believed others saw them, mattered greatly to how they influenced others. How they performed their leadership roles emanated from force of character aligned to core values. And, as revealed through their collective reflections, the interviewees perceived their leadership character to be predominently *humble, passionate,* and *contemplative* in character.

Humble

The interviewed leaders portrayed themselves as a humble lot. They were certainly not humbled, however, by any sense of inadequacy. They all had ample and just reason to feel confident about their ability to lead and otherwise contribute within their respective roles. Rather, the humility referenced in reflections about the character of their leadership performance conveyed a sense of service to a greater purpose and community. They were committed to serve a compelling purpose, and that, in turn, oriented them to serve others toward the achievement of that purpose. The interviewees were also appropriately humbled by the magnitude of moral responsibility that accompanied their leadership roles, as well as consciously committed to avoiding the perils of insolence and arrogance that too often afflict individuals in formal leadership positions.

> "The biggest threat to leadership is hubris."
>
> — *Patrick Sayne*

The 36 leaders were aware of their acknowledged leadership success, but at the same time, they consciously embraced humility. Perhaps this was so because most of them had not set out to be leaders. As Frank Lukasavitz noted, the role of leader was an unanticipated gift: "To be described as a leader is very uncomfortable for me. My life had humble beginnings, and I consider this a very rich ending."

Rather than planning for leadership, the interviewed leaders were pulled into their leadership roles by necessity and circumstance. Even many years after first assuming formal leadership roles and the attendant power and authority thereof, they remained humbled by their charge. Mechai Viraviadya phrased it this way: "The most important thing is not to take yourself too seriously. You are only one of six billion people on this planet, so you have to keep it in perspective and do the best that you can do." At the pinnacle of political power as Prime Minister of New Zealand, Helen Clark was very clear about that sentiment in describing her place in history: "I'm here because people have put their trust in me, not to rule the world."

While leadership itself can be intoxicating, Julianne Lowe was careful to warn against the siren call of power.

> I know that in roles like this, people put you up on a pedestal . . . if you are organizing things and leading a group. It is easy to start thinking of yourself that way. You have to be careful and not get carried away with yourself.

With the same cautionary note, Kuami Pianim admitted that it took some years to develop a humble perspective.

> When I was young I was taught that I was lucky and brilliant; as you get older you become humble. These talents have been given not only for yourself but to share and bring others up.

Most of the leaders conveyed clear understanding of their role as that of supporting the success of others, rather than seeking affirmation of self. Nola Hambleton was very insightful about the subtlety of her contributions to the success of others.

> You can be very self-deprecating and say, well, I'm not very good at this. There are days when I think, "Why is this day different than another? Why do I feel successful today when I didn't yesterday?" I guess I feel successful when I've negotiated something quietly or I've sown the seeds of an idea and seen it come to fruition . . . standing back and knowing that I've done something [and] that no one will probably know that [what] I've done has made a difference to someone.

Perhaps Richard Bissen best captured the leaders' appreciation for a humble perspective of self when he observed, "I take my job seriously, but I don't take myself seriously." This and many similar comments from the interviewed leaders spoke to a social sense of leadership virtue—a perception that their paramount leadership role was to serve the welfare of others.

Within their affirmation of humility, the interviewees also shared observations that further defined the dimensions of that general character trait. Specifically, they described the affiliated qualities of being *respectful, empathetic*, and *trustworthy*.

RESPECTFUL

The interviewed leaders were all highly respected by others for their leadership qualities. They, in turn, spoke forcefully about the importance of respecting others. Their position was that one was not likely to

> "I never want to disparage anyone."
>
> — Rod Chamberlain

be perceptively tuned in and empathetic to the wants and needs of others if there was not also an underlying element of respect. Leotis Watson did not mince words about his approach to the issue: "You ask anyone and they will say that I respect them." Leotis also observed that this simple rule kept him grounded in his fundamental values. "I have a foundation for myself, to treat everyone fairly as I would want to treated. It gives me the direction that I need."

Gavan Flick, the only Aboriginal art dealer in Sydney, Australia, was passionate about the importance of respect toward others.

> This community was built on respect. Every book written about us [Aboriginal people] describes a nomadic people. But we didn't just get up and walk into someone else's home. We couldn't do that. Just as today you wouldn't go into the neighbor's yard and use their pool or barbecue. You would have to be invited. Everything in our life was based on respect. You grew up respecting one another, the elders. Respect is also earned—you have to do the right thing to earn it. It's a two-way street.

Gavan talked at length about the need to treat his customers, employees, and the artists he represented with the respect that he felt they all deserved. Bob Knight applied a similar outlook in the corporate setting.

> I don't treat them like an employee. I don't refer to them as my worker, but rather as my associates. We are doing this together.

In moving from a corporate culture to a university position, John Hood not only held his new colleagues in high esteem but expected others to do so as well.

> Respect for the dignity of other people is very important to me. It doesn't matter who they are, what they are, what their views are. I think people here know that I am not tolerant of any participation by colleagues that isn't respectful. If someone doesn't want to participate in that type of forum, I drop the person's contribution gate very quickly.

A leadership disposition to be respectful is probably more easily exercised when business is running smoothly. The true test might come in a time of challenge and conflict. Don Hazelwood, Concertmaster for the Sydney Symphony, nurtured a deep sense of the worth of others, even in the most difficult of circumstances.

> Unpleasantries occur and you have to deal with them. I think you have to say the thing as you see it yourself. You've got to be diplomatic, but you have to couch it in terms that allow an opening for the person to avoid total embarrassment. You don't cut off a person's possibility of retreating from a situation. You can't cut off a person's dignity. That applies to everything in life, not just music. A person has to be approached if they are not reaching a certain standard, but they have to be allowed an opportunity to retreat from it in the most dignified manner that they can. Otherwise you are doing more damage than [good].

Working in a multinational, multicultural environment helped Brenda Schoonover prioritize the importance of conveying respect to others.

> During my early Peace Corps training, I learned that almost all cultures have the same value system, but it is the order in which those values are sometimes put that causes a lot of problems. Being sensitive to the culture and also respecting it is so important. The importance of respecting other cultures is something we need to take heed of, and show more sensitivity to, than some of us have done in the past.

Boon Yoon Chiang agreed:

> In Singapore, it is important to be sensitive to cultural traditions. I encourage everyone to bring part of their culture into the organization and to share their ideas.

In some instances, the character trait of being respectful was directly addressed through the proactive building of mutual understanding. In those instances, leaders actively cultivated and modeled mutual respect within their organizations. Mandy Macleod and CJ Nickerson used structured team-building processes to help employees understand each other better and develop more productive relationships. Mandy engaged her staff in a process called True Colors (Miscisin & Haines, 2001), a simplified personality type indicator to reveal and value strengths and differences within a group. CJ used the similar, but more sophisticated, Myers-Briggs personality type indicator (Kiersey & Bates, 1984). For both, the purpose was to build bridges of understanding and mutual respect, as well as to proactively minimize detrimental conflict.

Both overtly and covertly, the trait of being respectful to others emerged from the leaders' strong belief in the worth and dignity of all people, as well as from their commitment to be of humble service to others. Tim Brighouse exemplified this perspective in expressing confidence about the innate potential of human beings.

> I believe that most people have the capacity to do amazing things and that our job is to unlock what they can do. I want to make everyone feel special and unlock that potential.

Christine Rodriguez recognized that nevertheless, being respectful was a learned trait.

> One of the biggest lessons I have learned is that not everyone has the same drive, ambition, and work ethic that I have. In order to lead and motivate people, I have to accept that. I have learned to identify their strengths and weaknesses. I have had to learn to not be judgmental, because a good leader is not judgmental. You have to take the best and make the best of everyone.

EMPATHETIC

It would be difficult to respectfully engage others toward the achievement of goals if one were not attuned to both the overt and covert cues employed in human communication. Notably, most of the 36 leaders saw themselves as fairly perceptive of, and thereby responsive to, other people. Leotis Watson suggested that such was the case, when he observed, "I pay attention to everyone and everything." Julianne Lowe, nevertheless, thought that there might be some gender differences in such ability.

> "I try to keep in mind where everyone is coming from."
>
> — *Beth Stevenson*

> I think women are better at this. They notice things: a new haircut, a shirt someone is wearing. I had two ladies on this trip that stayed on the coach, and one had a hearing loss. I told her about my audiology training and she was delighted, and I could sense her thinking, "Oh, she understands." It's finding something that lets them know that you know how they think or that you think they are special. In nursing, you learn to pay attention. You can read what's going on, so you can connect with them. They may say they are fine, but they are not fine at all. To me, it is very important to understand what's worrying them; then you can unwind that and they know you can recognize it—they melt somehow.

It is obviously important for politicians to pay attention to what others are communicating about their wants and needs. Helen Clark was aware that she "had developed a good sense of what people feel." How else, she observed, could she hope to effectively serve their perceived interests? John Hood agreed, in stating that he had honed "a lifelong 'other' sense" and "purposely studied people closely." Whether through personal conversation, observation, or, as Richard Bissen put it, just an intuitive disposition to "pay attention to the details," the interviewed leaders saw themselves as characteristically perceptive about people. It was a trait that they prized highly and worked overtly to develop. Moreover, it reflected a cultivated social capacity for empathy.

Empathy, the ability to put oneself in another's shoes and know what they are thinking and feeling, moved the leaders beyond superficial perception of what was going on in others' heads or what messages were being communicated. This was a social instinct that enabled them to identify with the perceptions and experiences of others at a deeper level.

In presenting themselves as empathetic, the interviewed leaders described how that leadership trait benefited others. Kuami Pianim spent 10 years as a political prisoner. That experience reinforced his appreciation for the importance of empathy as a means to connect with other people.

> You need to live not too far away from people. I realized in prison that when you are talking to a person, they must realize that you are not too far away from the problem. If you cannot have empathy, you cannot be a good politician.

On a pragmatic level, Rod Chamberlain realized the value of empathy to his leadership perception that no one, including him, had all the answers and that most people were doing their very best to make worthy contributions to the cause. "I try to have conversation to create understanding both ways."

Beth Stevenson admired the empathetic character of one of her mentors and emulated those qualities herself.

> One of my mentors was a master at creating a network of belonging. She talked to everyone. I try to keep in mind where everyone is coming from. I believe that people are trying to do good. So matching individual techniques to individual people and your purpose is the best.

Empathy might be misinterpreted as a "soft" aspect of leadership and therefore not be fully appreciated. Fanny Law, Secretary for Education and Manpower for Hong Kong, addressed this perception with a moving example.

> People would characterize me as sometimes sentimental. I tend to have a soft spot for the disadvantaged. People would say that I sometimes would not hold the rules so strictly, but exercise more flexibility and discretion. There was a major accident on the third day of the Chinese New Year when I was Commissioner of Transport, and a bus overturned. A lady, who was the sole owner of the minibus, became comatose as a result. The license was up for renewal and under the law, the commissioner had no discretion to renew it on her behalf. I had very clear advice from the legal department, but the family depended on that license for their living. The father was also hurt, and there were three children. I asked the eldest boy to bring me a copy of the marriage and birth certificates to prove his identity, and we made the change [in the license renewal] so they were able to keep their business.

This example is all the more noteworthy in the context of the traditional Chinese bureaucracy, which is notoriously thick with rules and regulations that are to be followed to the letter.

The ability to sincerely identify with other people was seen by many of the leaders as a strong social relationship asset. Richard Bissen remarked on the importance of this skill.

> When I look across at a jury, they are just like my family . . . like my relatives. So I know what they want to hear. I know how to talk to them. I can think like the criminal too. I know what it's like to run around and be a rascal too. Culturally, I could not hold myself above or apart. I was trained to be very respectful and give deference to adults. I've been there—had the lowliest of the low jobs, I can think like them. . . . I can get into someone else's skin.

TRUSTWORTHY

Trustworthiness was strongly advocated by the 36 interviewed leaders. True to their commitment to humbly serve others in pursuit of a compelling purpose, they were both respectful and empathetic in their interactions with people. They also worked hard to build trust in their organizations.

> "My word is my bond. If you don't have trust and integrity, you cannot lead."
>
> —John Hood

Ian Fox did not equivocate on this matter: "I'm always honest and open. It's vital that staff has faith in leadership." Richard Bissen let his colleagues know "that life isn't fair, but I am. If they feel that they have gotten slighted, they can come to me and I will be fair. I don't play favorites." Mandy Macleod echoed a similar sentiment in stating, "I treat people fairly and equally; there are no favorites here." As Gabor Halmai explained, however, exercising this trait sometimes comes with a price.

> The prior president had kept special funds for discretionary use, not reviewed by the board. I abolished the special money. This wasn't easy, due to special cases that do arise. But I think it is important that no special treatment or favors are given. The past recipients were not happy.

Several of the interviewed leaders also observed that authenticity is integral to trustworthiness. Julianne Lowe related that "you have to be genuine [because] everyone recognizes a phony. . . . I used to tell my sons that everyone loves flattery, but it has got to be real." That people would trust a leader and confide in them was similarly important. Boon Yoon Chiang commented on this in relation to his efforts to build a trusting environment.

> I think they trust me. They feel that I can weigh whatever they bring to me and look at it objectively. If it is the right thing, they know that I'll come back to them and say, "This is the right thing to do, and you should be doing it." If it is not, I think they know that I would come back to them and give a proper explanation as to why it isn't the right thing to do. That trust must be there; otherwise, you will dampen their spirit.

Chet Bradley described how he worked to build trust in the early stages of a developing relationship.

> I usually tell people, if they want to listen, quite a bit about me. I reveal myself to you and if you haven't met with me before, I hope to get information back about you. From there, I try to carve that personal relationship into some professional role that will help us act on what needs to be done to achieve our goal.

Greenleaf (1996) observed that the servant leader's role is to leave others more empowered and otherwise better off than when the leader first encountered them. Many of the interviewed leaders observed that the building of trusting relationships over time communicated authentic belief in the positive potential of others. As Bob Knight observed, however, trust takes time to build and can be withdrawn in a second.

> You have to build trust over time. [But] like a rubber band that you wind tighter and tighter by what you say and what you do, it can be unwound in a day. And then it is very hard to rebuild.

Without such characteristic commitment to building and sustaining trust, any leadership influence of consequence is doubtful. Helen Clark wasted few words in describing the bottom line of why a servant leader needs to continually work on a trusting relationship: "Trust can be withdrawn. . . . I serve at the will of the people."

Passionate

Humble servants that they professed to be, the 36 leaders nevertheless described themselves as characteristically very aware of and committed to their passions. They were always focusing themselves and those they

> "I have a core passion for my mission."
>
> —*John Hood*

served in a straightforward manner on important matters that warranted meaningful attention. They were also both tough and vulnerable in their championing of compelling purpose.

The passionate fervor the leaders felt for their life callings was evident across all 36 interviews. Frank Lukasavitz described his calling this way: "I consider teaching not a job, but a privilege." All the leaders spoke with great emotion about what they did and why they did it. CJ Nickerson, for example, was so passionate about the creation of a new foundation for promoting health education for children that he made sure no personal profit came to him.

> I didn't want to cause people not to trust my work, not to trust the program, which ultimately was good for kids. I wanted to insure that [the initial program] would reach the market because it was of such high quality.

Likewise, Mechai Viravaidya decided not to take any salary from the Population Development Association (PDA) that he leads. He chose instead to live modestly off a slice of his inheritance, one third of which he also gave to the PDA.

The heartfelt passions the leaders shared were obviously aligned to beliefs within their core value system. Fanny Law articulated such deeply held beliefs:

> I believe that everyone is born with the motivation to learn. Every child is born with the curiosity to learn and explore. Every child has the ability to

learn, but they may move at different paces, and everyone has the right and deserves the opportunity learn. So these are the three fundamental principles that underlie the philosophy of the entire education reform in Hong Kong. We want to build a more inclusive, more equitable system, [one that] goes against the grain of the traditional Chinese culture.

Fanny's case was similar to the experiences of the other interviewed leaders, in that her orientation to a passionate value position sustained her through many tough challenges.

Several interviewed leaders commented on the benefits of revealing their passion to others. Richard Bissen described a frequent reaction that he would get from jurors of his trial work.

> A juror in one of my trials asked me [after the trial] if I was related to the victims. They said I acted like I was related to them. "You argue as if they were your friend." [That's why] I have never handled a case that I don't believe in.

Passion was often described by the 36 leaders as emerging from compelling purpose. As Christine Rodriguez explained, "I am passionate about the education focus of our philanthropy. My only regret is that I can't do more. I really enjoy what I am doing." Michael Barber was also aware of a strong value connection to passion.

> I've talked about my obsession with work and my commitment to my passion. It's not just about systems design. The thing that makes me driven is making a difference for the people in the community. If it wasn't about real change on the ground, I wouldn't do the things I do.

As was the case in their prior reflections about elements within their affinity for humility, the interviewed leaders also described several traits that served their passionate character. They spoke in particular about the traits of being *focused*, *straightforward*, and *tough*.

FOCUSED

The interviewed leaders observed that they were continuously focused by their sense of values and purpose as they went about their daily business or planned for the future.

> "Values are the core of the organization and become the touchstone for decision making."
>
> —Beth Stevenson

Many of the leaders described how they used their core values as a touchstone for focusing their leadership efforts. As Christine Rodriguez noted, the values formed in childhood provide a foundation for the way one sees oneself as a leader.

My parents were spiritual leaders for me and of high moral character. The qualities I have and the beliefs that I hold are very well grounded in what I learned from them.

While talking about her values related to her commitment to the at-risk student population she served, Jeanne Dukes observed:

You have to believe that the kids will survive . . . that life is really hard, but they will survive and are salvageable. If you believe that they are, you will treat them that way. You have to believe that they are smart enough to catch on, which they are. You have to believe in the value and quality of the kids. . . . Even though they might look ragged and might talk ragged and have been raised by wolves, the next generation will be better because of what we are doing. You have to believe in the worth of our cause, of the worth of these kids.

Another educator, Gary Rasmussen, also felt strongly about how his value orientation toward students provided direction for his decision making. "I have a nonnegotiable commitment to kids, above all else."

In seeing themselves as the keeper of a value vision, these leaders understood their responsibility to be one of staying the course and not getting pulled off line by the many distractions that came their way. Rod Chamberlain observed:

I am a steward for this organization, and I have a responsibility to achieve those goals. I have to use my discernment and check it out to be sure that I am not off the wall, but I will then follow through day to day.

Beth Stevenson was very aware of the challenge of staying centered amid the flood of leadership tasks.

I never lose sight of what I am trying to accomplish. There is always so much going on and so many distractions. For me, success is a calling, and it is not just the mission, but how you get there. The core values are the touchstone, and we use them as a continuous yardstick. Ultimately, I look inside. Can I live with myself? Am I ethically accomplishing my core purpose?

To avoid becoming distracted by the inevitable myriad activities within daily schedules, Roger Harmon suggested that a leader necessarily had to take in the whole picture.

One has to pay attention to self, individuals, and the complexity of the situation, from the foreground to the background, from the immediate to the broader context. It involves not just trying to get somewhere by assisting other people, but seeing what it is that I can contribute as well.

Some of the leaders prescribed specific strategies for maintaining focus on what is important in the midst of distraction and competing tasks. Gary Rasmussen, for example, adopted a process to help him and his organization focus their efforts.

> We use total quality management principles around a problem. Once we've accomplished our goals, we try to maintain the progress and not let it slip; then we'll move on to the next challenge.

In order to sustain focus, Gary continued,

> We really have to keep it in the forefront. It has to be the top [leadership] modeling what we do, as well as reinforcing and following up; otherwise, it will die a slow death.

Beth Stevenson described a similar affinity to process as a means to focus.

> I try to be centered, because there is always so much going on and so many distractions. If you can distill things down to clear steps, you avoid fragmentation. Creating a good process is critical in order to allow for ambiguity, but keeping the focus [is also critical] so those things keep moving.

Leotis Watson used another approach to maintaining focus, that of modeling it for others.

> Everyone knows Leotis because they know that I respect everyone and lead by example. To me, the key is consistency. They see it and hear it day in and day out. I am trying to perfect a way in myself that through performance on a consistent basis, they see this guy is doing the same thing every day in every way.

Mandy Macleod concurred with such need for action that was aligned to purpose: "You not only have to be visionary, but you have to be seen doing it."

STRAIGHTFORWARD

Clarity and passion about core values formed early in life promotes leadership that is straightforward and open in character. Fanny Law traced such character in herself to her family's influence.

> "I'm always honest and open. It's vital that staff has faith in leadership."
>
> —Ian Fox

My father is a fairly straightforward person. He has this character with this company. . . . He is seen as a no-nonsense manager. As a civil servant, I also am much more [inclined toward] straight talk. So I think I inherited this from my father.

Similarly, Christine Rodriguez noted the genesis of such a trait.

The value for honesty came from my parents. They have always instilled that in us. I don't want to sound like I'm way up there, but for the most part, I do carry on my life with honesty and candor.

Kuami Pianim and Patrick Sayne talked about the importance of honesty in creating a psychologically safe environment for others. Kuami noted the value orientation to honesty he received from his grandmother.

She taught us to be honest and don't tell a lie. When you tell a lie, you have to remember it. When you speak the truth, you don't need to remember it because it is a part of you.

Patrick applied the same value to his leadership role.

You have to be authentic and honest. No game playing. You can't let people get the impression that they are being handled or manipulated. That's where the honesty comes in. There is no [apparent] risk in saying it, but I'm not going to say I will consider something when I mean no. That will also kill open discourse as fast as any type of humiliation.

Richard Bissen described his aversion to game playing as well and talked about the fact that he could detect it because at one time, he played those games himself.

I've become a performer, but I used to be a heckler. I know when someone is playing with me and I say, "Never bullshit a bullshitter."

Whether eloquent or pragmatic, the message from the interviewed leaders was consistent: If people are to trust leaders, they must perceive them as passionately honest and forthright. When manipulation and game playing are discouraged, people will know where they stand and feel free to contribute their opinions and ideas openly.

One of the ways in which the leaders invited straightforward interactions was to open themselves up to others. Roger Harmon described it this way:

I think you have to be willing to be vulnerable with people and let them have a pretty good insight into what I am seeing as the dynamics of the situation. I don't hold the cards very close to my vest. I get a lot of advice, and share my own experience, but always in relation to the goals of the organization.

Although he was close to the main seat of governmental power in Great Britain, Michael Barber was similarly willing to expose his vulnerability.

I spend a lot of time here with the staff, but I also spend a lot of time on Downing Street. About 2 weeks ago, I was worrying about a number of things, and I did what all leadership books tell you not to do, which is just share a set of worries with the team without having any resolution. So on that occasion, I shared with them, and we've now been through it, and we've sort of come to a resolution and [Prime Minister] Blair's on board for what I want to do for the next phase. In one way, that was bad leadership, but I think it helped to convey a message on how you involve people in [the process].

As John Hood described it, moreover, being straightforward and open with others also means that one has to follow that path in dealing with the consequences.

I recently showed anger in a meeting and spent the morning going around and apologizing to all present. I am always prepared to learn from my mistakes and genuinely apologize for them.

It appeared, then, that the leaders sought to balance straightforward approachability and openness with an unwavering focus on the accomplishment of purpose. Fanny Law's observation captured that balancing act.

I constantly have to remind myself to see things from the other side. I invite the other side from all of my colleagues—I invite them to speak the truth to me. Sometimes, [however,] people will find the soft options. I always tell my colleagues that we must focus our attentions on the interests of the students.

TOUGH

Passionately focused and straightforward, the 36 leaders also opined about the importance of maintaining an internal toughness and resilience.

Fanny Law elaborated on balancing a straightforward and open relationship with associates with a tough stance on fundamental issues.

> "What makes a successful organization is sticking to a few key values."
>
> —*Patrick Sayne*

I go out very often to meet frontline educators. I go to schools every week at 7:30 in the morning. It keeps me in touch with reality. In fact, I am the person who has mixed reputations. People say I am very approachable, that I listen. But I can also be a taskmaster and can, at times, be stern in dealing with staff and business associates.

Many of the leaders expressed the need to maintain some emotional distance at the same time they were cultivating strong open relationships. Julianne Lowe called it putting on the shop face.

I grew up in a shop. My parents had a grocery store. . . . We were dealing with people and we could be having a fight out back and then the bell would ring, and we would rush up with big smiles on our faces and say, "Good morning how can I help you?" I learned to cover my inner emotions. You could be angry inside and then put on your shop face.

Relating this attribute to her current work, Julianne further noted:

You do toughen up in this job or you could lose your faith in mankind. You can't get too personally involved. If you get too close or too friendly, they start to see you as the same as them with the same sort of faults and then they stop trusting your leadership and start doubting you. Others will resent it as well if you get too close.

Mandy Macleod concurred with that perspective in talking about learning the skill of appearing calm when emotions are broiling under the surface.

I am even tempered on the surface. I think it is very much something you have to be when you deal with people. They need to see calmness; they don't want to see you losing your temper. They don't want to see you dissolving into tears, and if you have to do these things, you do it in private. I think the face of an administrator can oftentimes be very different from what is really on the inside.

Some might judge such self-management of emotions to be inauthentic, yet John Hood was firm on the need for such toughness.

You have to do it. I mean you could call that disingenuous, but it is not intended to be. It is done in one's interpretation of the best interest of the organization at that point in time.

Patrick Sayne described learning a similar lesson.

I've learned not to let my hot button get pushed. There is a certain kind of play-acting in leadership. You have to hide it when you are angry. But you have to put it in perspective. I tell people when they get upset, "You need to understand that as long as school opens in the morning and there is a teacher to meet those students . . . not a hell of lot can happen that is really bad." In the scheme of things, that's what is really important. You figure out that the sun is going to rise in the east no matter what happens. You don't want to give up, but you want to adopt an attitude that there is always another day.

A dramatic example of leadership toughness in the face of a challenge to core values came from Leotis Watson, who, as a head concierge, was always in the public eye.

One guest got irate about some tickets that she thought were too expensive. I said I would call and try to get a reduction on price. At one point in the heated exchange she said, "Well isn't that just like a nigger." The other guests watched for my reaction. I thought, "That may be how you feel, but it can't harm me." I refuse to let anybody or anything turn that attitude around. If anything, I am going to turn them around. Whenever you are working, you're on stage. It is up to each one of us to make it happen.

The interviewed leaders often observed that asserting one's beliefs could advance one's purpose, but that it also took courage to do so. Brenda Schoonover recalled instances when being a woman in a leadership position put her at a disadvantage.

I had to fight not only for housing [in a posting in Tanzania] but also for an equal portfolio [work assignment] that the men there had. I learned to approach it with a positive attitude and assume that everybody was up front. So I spoke out in a firm, calm manner. I think if I had gotten hysterical, they probably would've put me on the next plane out of there.

The leaders also commented on the importance of managing personal stress to the advantage of their leadership influence on their organizations. Bob Knight, for example, described how he learned to adopt a tough approach to managing his own emotions in order to reduce stress on himself and others.

I am part German and [part] Irish. When I was very young, things could get me upset. I learned to understand what stress is all about. It's all inside. The experience is what is it, but it's how you interpret it. You have to control it. In the end, you have to be able to let it slide. It took me several years to hold it in and not let it blow. When I watched other leaders blow up, they looked like fools and were hurting themselves and losing respect.

Contemplative

The 36 leaders collectively portrayed themselves as humble servants who were passionately committed to achieving compelling purpose. They also described themselves as characteristically contemplative about purpose and how best to achieve it. They were, in a word, thinkers. It was their manner to ponder what was necessary and possible to do. They were given to reflective analysis of the way things were, as well as what might be. Furthermore, the reflections of the interviewed leaders presented such musings as natural and

> "Effective [organizations] have something that draws them together, to discuss, debate, and challenge, and the vision develops."
>
> —Ian Fox

necessary to their decision-making and problem-solving responsibilities. As Frank Lukasavitz put it, "I have always been a rebel. I question everything." Such contemplative character was most evident in the leaders' accounts of their propensity to be visionary and meditative in performing their leadership roles.

VISIONARY

The importance of formulating an orienting organizational vision is ubiquitous in the leadership literature (Bass, 1998; Kouzes & Posner, 1995; Sashkin, 2003). The interviewed leaders certainly had no argument with that time-honored perspective. Alex Banful, for example, spoke of learning early in life about the importance of cultivating a clear vision of the future.

> "Leaders must know the way, show the way, and go the way."
>
> —Mandy Macleod

> My father used to say that he was building our houses in his head, as he planned for our future. That's what I find myself saying now, take the house in your head and build it in the way you want. I have built this organization from 1 1/2 people to the 82 we employ now. I can see the long haul.

John Hood concurred that the cultivation of a common vision was an essential and ongoing leadership responsibility.

> I think anyone in an organizational leadership position has to have an eye over the horizon, as well as an eye immediately on the land in front. One has to be constantly thinking about where the world is going, how the university world is developing internationally, what are the things we need to be thinking about as an institution to ensure that we remain in the upper league, what are the directions we need to be pursuing, and then use the organizational process to test and evolve it.

Patrick Sayne observed that envisioning the future was a unique responsibility of leadership: "I think a manager is someone who provides organization, but a leader provides vision." Gabor Halmai spoke of the importance of leadership attention to the big picture of what the organization was about and how it would conduct its business. When he assumed his leadership role with a foundation, he was faced with redefining the mission and streamlining the organization to better serve that mission.

> I think the most important thing is to find out the mission and the tools to fulfill it. I came here to change the functioning of the organization, to concentrate on some really important things. We need to concentrate on policy issues and work on cultural issues. We [the board and I] decide on the most important guidelines, and then there are no problems.

Rod Chamberlain reflected about the indigenous value for envisioning the future, as he described the Hawaiian custom of investing for future generations.

> One of the strengths of the Hawaiian culture is the *ali'i*, or the chiefs, and how they look to the future. In fact, for them, the culture was to look ahead not one generation, not two, but seven generations into the future. They would judge a decision of an *ali'i* based on what would happen seven generations or 140 years from now. If you look around, that is what has happened here. This is the first permanent K–12 campus since the original on Oahu in 1877 . . . so we think this a part of that original vision that Bernice Polahi Bishop had for Kamehameha schools and for Hawaii. This belief in planning for future generations is held to be important not only in the Hawaiian culture, but in many other indigenous cultures as well, and has had a profound effect on the development of many leaders.

On a national political level, Helen Clark described the essentials of an influential vision: "You must believe in the mission yourself and have ideas and values that people can identify with." Helen further noted the importance of keeping the vision in the forefront. "You have to create the agenda and keep moving forward. If you're moving, you're a very hard target. I look forward, never back."

The interviewed leaders also perceived a need to align vision with values. To that end, they most often connected their personal goals and sense of purpose to their vision for their organization. Patrick Sayne illustrated this orientation.

> My central core is honesty, directness, and integrity. Our job is to serve the kids. Anything outside of that is peripheral. You can lead through deceit and manipulation, but that is not leading—it's controlling. Even with good values you can lose your position, but with the negative ones you absolutely will.

Ian Fox thought the concept of aligning values and vision to be rather straightforward.

> I don't think it's too difficult really; it's just reminding occasionally, if we have a difficult decision to make, then maybe we go back to that core belief [that] it's paramount that the focus is on students first.

Developing a sense of coherence between values and vision and practice was a theme that often emerged within the interviews. Michael Barber, for example, described the effect of writing about his vision.

> I wrote a book called *The Learning Game* about my vision of how the education system should be. I still draw from it. . . . When you write your vision down, you have to deal with that. It brings coherence to the way you approach things. That was absolutely seminal for me.

Along this line, several leaders commented on the necessity of stepping back and seeing the organization as a whole, rather than getting tied up in the day-to-day minutia. Mechai Viravaidya, for example, observed that he worked to see the whole and the parts simultaneously by planning systemically and operating pragmatically. He further commented that "refusing to accept defeat forces you to look at the whole." Beth Stevenson had yet another take on building community and connecting everyday practice to values and vision within an organization.

> I always try to work more holistically and feel successful when I have helped somebody do something to broaden their horizons or build their skills. I keep asking myself, "What can I do to help to make a person's life easier and the organization work better?" I try to avoid fragmentation. People need to see the whole so they have a sense of belonging and sense of team. We create a sense of community when we see ourselves within the big picture. We create a comfort level when what we do is aligned with our values.

Suffice it to say, the interviewed leaders believed in the necessity and power of vision. Mandy Macleod succinctly captured the essence of their sentiments.

> You have to have a vision. You have to be able to lead to the vision. And you have to show the people how to come along with you. Leaders must know the way, show the way, and go the way.

MEDITATIVE

Beyond their contemplative visioning of ultimate destinations, the interviewed leaders also mentally massaged the details of how to get there. From the reflections they shared, it was not that they would stop and think things over every great once in a while; rather, they were almost in a continuous meditative state where they habitually thought things through either on the run or in structured opportunities for reflection. Both intuitively and from their experience, they had developed a strong value for thinking about what they were doing before, during, and after doing it.

> "I'm always trying to figure out how to do something better. I keep asking myself what I can do to help make a person's life easier and the organization work better."
>
> —Beth Stevenson

Nola Hambleton, for example, observed that she learned about the value of prior reflection from early life experiences with doing things first and asking questions later. Now more experienced and wiser, she commented, "I now see the end before moving forward." Rod Chamberlain spoke of a mentor's influence on his acquiring a deeper appreciation for a meditative approach to leadership performance.

> One of my mentors is a Quaker, and he refined my thinking about how to help others. The Quaker process of clarification is very affirming and deeply reflective.

Many of the leaders structured time and space for meditating (i.e., thinking deeply) about multiple issues associated with their leadership responsibilities and interests. Ross Gilbert viewed such reflection as necessary to his daily survival.

> I sit over there [pointing to a spot in his office]. I purposefully change my space in the office and sit and reflect. Sometimes I read and sometimes I write in my diary on the day's activities. I think about them and what I am going to do and how I'm going to carry through my basic principles of action during the day.

Highly visible leaders like Helen Clark and John Hood were clear about the need to take the time to think through their agendas. Helen shared that "I take a month in the summer to read, organize, and plan the PM statement in the fall." Likewise, John had learned to annually schedule a concentrated time for thinking things through.

> I generally spend the summer vacation thinking very long and hard. In each of the three years I've done that now, the action plan that comes out the other end is very close to the agenda that I've thought through while on leave.

Several of the leaders talked about often experiencing external pressures to rush to judgment—and their determination not to let that happen. Mandy Macleod described her resistance strategy.

> I need to feel sure that I've come up with the best solution because I'm not comfortable with failure. I like to think that what I'm aiming at is going to be successful because I've given it enough thought to make it as successful as possible. Often I say, "I will get back to you." If it's pressing, "I'll get back to you in a half hour."

Helen Clark, given the magnitude of her government responsibilities, was very adamant about adequately thinking through an issue. "I refuse to make judgments under pressure. I like to establish my own rhythm in my work and grab the timetable."

And understandably, the interviewees, like all leaders who are committed to achieving a meaningful purpose, were adverse to failure. This did not mean, however, that they did not view mistakes and missteps as learning opportunities. CJ Nickerson, for example, noted that he had developed a natural tendency to process the "what" and "how" of things gone wrong.

> I learn a lot of different ways, but I try to learn from my mistakes. There is self-analysis. . . . Right after a mistake, I may be in a clean-up mode, but then I'll find myself pulling weeds in the garden thinking about it. These things tend to stay with me.

Lessons Learned

When asked to describe defining qualities of their leadership performance, these 36 leaders observed the importance of leadership character. Their collective reflections suggest that their leadership performance was necessarily in character because it emanated from their core values. How they performed was prefaced by who they were as defined by what they believed and held to be most important.

In describing attributes of their leadership character, the interviewed leaders shared the essence of *who* they perceived themselves to be. In their minds, the way they saw themselves and how others saw them was a significant element of how they performed to influence others toward the achievement of goals.

The prominent perceptions of leadership performance shared by this particular group of leaders to this point, then, appear to be the following:

1. Leadership performance emanates from force of character aligned to values.

2. Leadership benefits from performance that is humble, passionate, and contemplative in character.

Regarding the leaders' perception that leadership performance emanates from character aligned to values, it is a difficult position to argue against. First and foremost, how the 36 leaders saw it is how they saw it. It was their perception. That they so strongly and collectively observed the importance of such alignment, however, warrants our further attention. This is a particularly important observation to the degree that it suggests how coherent leadership, that is, leadership defined by natural and logical relationships between essential elements, evolves (see Figure 5.1).

The leaders' awareness of a force of character within their leadership performance is encouraging to the current resurgence of leadership trait research (Lowe & Gardner, 2000). As to their collective endorsement of particular leadership character traits, it obviously falls once more into the province of

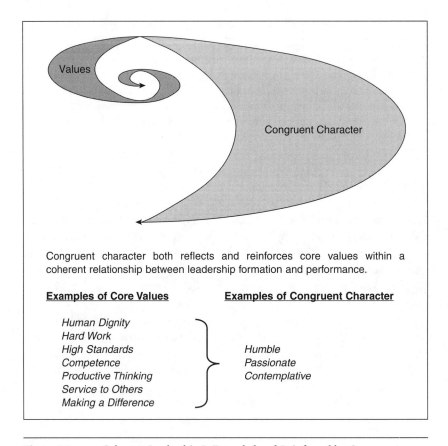

Congruent character both reflects and reinforces core values within a coherent relationship between leadership formation and performance.

Examples of Core Values   **Examples of Congruent Character**

Human Dignity
Hard Work
High Standards   *Humble*
Competence   *Passionate*
Productive Thinking   *Contemplative*
Service to Others
Making a Difference

Figure 5.1   Coherent Leadership Is Extended and Reinforced by Congruent Character

personal experience and perception. Again, however, the prominence of the character traits of humility, passion, and contemplation across the stories shared by these 36 leaders warrants respect for the collective wisdom offered. Furthermore, the character observations of the interviewed leaders find reinforcement in the leadership literature. Greenleaf (1996), for example, espouses the virtues of the Servant Leader, and Collins (2001) provides additional perspective of humble leadership from his description of the Level Five Leader. Regarding leaders being characteristically passionate, where is the successful leader, we might ask, who is not passionate about his or her purpose? That is, if you think of a leader of historical stature, they were passionate about their cause, right? Fullan (2003) and Leider (1997) speak to the importance of a strong orientation to compelling purpose. Goleman, Boyatzis, and McKee (2002) add their insights about the emotional dynamic behind Primal

Leadership. In the matter of contemplation, who is going to advocate for leaders who don't think about what they are doing or why or how they are doing it? But should the position need support, Covey (1989), Perkins (1995), and Gardner (1995) describe the qualities and benefits of good thinking habits.

Further Conversation

With the previously mentioned insights in mind, we move on, in Chapter 6, to further reflection about leadership performance—reflections that describe how leadership performance was acted out across prominent fields of behavior. Before we do so, however, you are invited to engage in Exercises 5.1 and 5.2.

EXERCISE 5.1   Further Conversation: Force of Character

With reference to your prior reflection in Further Conversation Exercise 2.1:

A. What are the core values that orient your approach to life and leadership?

B. What character traits define how you see yourself as a leader?

C. What character traits define how others see you as a leader?

D. How are your leadership character traits congruent with your core values?

EXERCISE 5.2

A. Why might congruency between leadership values and character matter?

B. Why might humility be a valuable force of character in leadership performance?

C. Why might passion be a valuable force of character in leadership performance?

D. Why might contemplation be a valuable force of character in leadership performance?

E. What is the single most important character trait of an effective leader? Why?

6

Acted Out

How does individual behavior aggregate to collective behavior?

—Watts (2003, p. 24)

Performed Across Fields of Behavior

Characters come alive on stage and screen by the actions of actors. Similarly, defining qualities of human character emerge on the stage of life through the actions of real people in real-world contexts. Thus, as Ulice Payne observed, "The ultimate manifestation of leadership is in the act."

The 36 interviewed leaders were real people who performed leadership roles across diverse reality contexts. In reflecting about the force of character behind their performance, they perceived themselves to be characteristically humble, passionate, and contemplative in carrying out their leadership roles. Their further reflection revealed that they were also accomplished actors who, by their actions, translated leadership character into compatible leadership behavior. Such behavior, by their accounts, was prominently performed across the three fields of *community building, centering,* and *thinking.*

Community Building

Given their characteristic embrace of humble service to others in pursuit of compelling purpose, it is not surprising that the interviewed leaders described behaving in ways that targeted the building of viable communities. Indeed, the leaders' affinity for community building was notably aligned to their bias toward respectful, empathetic, and trustworthy relationships. It was from such force of character that the leaders acted to organize teams that would be up to the task of achieving meaningful purpose. During interview reflections about how they carried out their leadership roles, the leaders frequently observed that if compelling purpose were to be adequately served, it would take a viable village to serve it. To that end, they described leadership behaviors intended to build communities in which everyone was on the same page, supported, and ready and able to get the job done. Among the numerous community-building actions described in the interviews, the leaders were particularly observant of behaviors that *acclimated*, *matched*, *empowered*, and *teamed* community members.

> "While the organization's mission is central, at the end of the day, what happens between people is where the richness is. The extent to which things move is the extent to which we have created a community."
>
> — *Beth Stevenson*

ACCLIMATING

The interviewed leaders consistently described their leadership performance in terms of behaviors that acclimated members to a safe, supportive, and committed organizational climate. Creating a safe culture within the organization was viewed not only as a means to an end, but as significant in and of itself. Bob Knight took pride in establishing such a culture at Paul Homes.

> "I want them to know that the organization cares. The organization listens."
>
> — *Alex Banful*

There is great camaraderie within the company, a great respect for each other's ability and what they do. Now, it's like a family, so don't think it is always perfect. We have our momentary blips. The big thing is that this group really respects and enjoys each other. They laugh and joke together. If I have a section that is pouting, I see what's going on and then redirect them.

The 36 leaders conveyed proactive concern for establishing a positive emotional climate for those they led, as well as for themselves. Rich Teerlink talked about working hard to "set a tone where people can say, 'It's nice to be in a place where we don't have to be careful.'"

The task, as the leaders generally saw it, was to build productive working relationships and strong bonds of mutual caring while maintaining a focus on the mission at hand. Beth Stevenson asserted that the end goal was that "we have a shared sense of humanity." Richard Bissen's take was that "we are a family and we are a business, but we are not a family business." He made it clear within his office of 28 lawyers and myriad support personnel that it was important to maintain a caring community concern for one another. At the same time, he continually reminded his associates that their ultimate mission was to serve, protect, and defend the citizens of Maui County. Rod Chamberlain seemed to agree when sharing his sense of community. "I like the sense of community rather than family. There is a set of relationships in family, but in community you also have tasks that have to be done . . . and it is why we are here."

Many of the leaders talked of working to structure a sense of community within their organizations. Mechai Viraviadya described the egalitarian tradition of the Population Development Association (PDA).

> We have 25-year relationships here and an egalitarian structure. In the tough times, we froze everyone's salary so that no one had to be fired. I have a fierce loyalty to those who have made the commitment to work here and they all know it. We work as a team.

The egalitarian climate that Mechai described was observable to those who visited PDA or the affiliated fund-raising restaurant next door, Condoms and Cabbages. As Mechai approached his employees, greetings were exchanged through the traditional Thai clasping of hands and bowing, a demonstration that communicated a deep and sincere sense of mutual respect and appreciation.

Alex Banful adopted a similar approach in creating a flat organizational structure at the nonprofit organization he founded.

> I have an open door. Everyone [here] has an open door. We don't put titles on the door. Titles have a way of making people feel. bigger than they actually are . . . especially if you have to move someone from one office to the other. Wisdom and knowledge is not in any one person's head.

CJ Nickerson described a cumulative approach to making associates feel like valued members of the organization.

> We tried to set a positive emotional climate. When people had to travel, we gave them credit cards, which conveys trust and doesn't cause them the stress of using their personal finances. We paid actual costs. We wanted them to be sure to stay in places they felt safe. We took care of families that were in need by gathering up stuff they needed. We kept staff meetings short. We celebrated birthdays.

Rod Chamberlain commented on the need for supportive communal structures in schools and other organizations.

> We are currently looking at the calendar to find time for teachers to get together across the grades. One thing I do as a leader is set the agenda. What are the issues that we are dealing with? So, by creating time for people to get together to exchange ideas and build on ideas, you need a facilitative process. You have to model an ongoing process and provide a time frame to allow this to happen.

Other leaders were also proactive in structuring time and opportunity for building productive relationships. Gary Rasmussen encouraged people to "intentionally schedule time for direct communication links [face to face]. . . . You have to be proactive about relationships, and with e-mail, it's too easy to do everything using technology." Julianne Lowe employed a variety of strategies to create and reorganize connections within groups. Her approach was to "try to get them all personally involved at some stage" because she believed that everyone would benefit and contribute more through a shared experience that valued their participation.

John Hood offered a very simple and direct approach to the promotion of productive community interaction: "If we are having a meeting with a large group, I will actually say at the beginning that what I am looking for is respectful, collegial dialogue and discourse."

Within such community acclimating behavior, there was a very apparent value reference, one that sincerely honored the dignity and potential of every member of the organization. This was a value that was both walked and talked within the shared accounts of the 36 leaders. Rich Teerlink spoke to this value perspective.

> The very glue of any organization starts with relationships. I worked with Max Dupree at Herman Miller and he always said, "Leaders, by their actions and not by their words, establish a sense of justice within the organization." You have to give everyone a right to their opinion.

Building one-on-one personal relationships with colleagues and employees was another avenue utilized in community building. CJ Nickerson characterized his leadership style as highly personal. Relationships within the Comprehensive Health Education Foundation (CHEF) were, in his eyes, paramount. "Every day I make a point to get a cup of coffee and walk around and talk to people . . . about their families, interests, concerns, or problems."

Leotis Watson, Ross Gilbert, Tim Brighouse, and Rod Chamberlain shared similar observations about connecting to people and letting them know that you truly cared. Leotis commented on the importance of connecting with people.

> Every day you shake their [the employees'] hand and ask, "How are you today and how do you feel?" It is so important to find out how they are doing at the beginning of their shift. They may not be feeling well or could have had a family crisis. A thousand and one things could have happened that would affect their day . . . so I give them the opportunity to say how they feel. My main concern is to show them that I care about them as a person first. If you feel the importance of their person, they feel the importance of their job.

Ross offered a compatible view in describing how he attended to personal contacts.

I go to the students' concerts because I love to see the other side of them; same with faculty. We hang out in the union having coffee most mornings. Because of the social contact, it's hard to think of any of them who haven't come to me at some time or another to ask about teaching or talk about problems.

Tim espoused a simple strategy that worked well for him: "I write personal notes to everyone at one time or another. I have written thousands of them over the years." Rod expressed appreciation for the importance of lasting impressions and follow-through in building community on a personal level.

There is a phrase here . . . to talk story . . . to tell a little about yourself . . . have a conversation and that's how it starts. I often end a workshop with faculty with an invitation to talk. Ending meetings with "What can I do to support you? What do you need?"

The interviewed leaders were also savvy about building and bridging supportive community networks both within and outside of their organizations. Rod Chamberlain cited McKay's (1996) *Swim With the Sharks* Rolodex strategy of never throwing away a business card.

When he [McKay] wrote his first book, he called everyone in [his rolodex]. So I try to do that and network, network, network. I try to mentor others to do this as well. How do you build networks with other people so you can pick up the phone and talk to them? It's not the career ladder anymore; it's the network. It's a way of getting people to new stages. There are so many people that don't realize how good they are. So I say, "Talk to so-and-so, give them a call." Or I call my colleagues and say, "I have this person I would like you to talk to." I try to help them make the connections.

In close step with their relationship-nurturing behaviors, the interviewed leaders also acted to affirm and celebrate community success. Indeed, letting others know that they were appreciated for their good work was paramount for many of the leaders. Bob Knight described the value of such affirmation.

Patting someone on the back and saying "good job" is worth a million dollars. I am very quick to praise, because people need approval. I need it. It makes you feel good, and everyone wants to do well. I never take credit for anything. I always give all the credit to the people who are working with me and praise their ideas. I think that is why I have been successful in bringing so many people to the company from my prior company. They wanted to come here to work with me.

Affirming the work of others was often tied to accomplishment of purpose, not just empty praise. Roger Harmon noted that he always affirmed positive intention.

I legitimize and cheer the small victories that people make. Peace Corps volunteers want to change the world, which is why they are here. What is more realistic are the little, everyday acts, consistent work towards relationship building and meeting manpower and technical needs; the small victories. Ultimately, people breathe a sigh of relief that the small victories are enough.

Within an educational setting, Ian Fox and Gary Rasmussen found ways to provide compliments in a meaningful way. Gary observed that "since education is without a career ladder, we offer challenges and excitement, encouragement and recognition for professionalism and learning." Ian made sure that praise was appropriately placed with those who did the work, not the leader.

Our school has received a reasonable amount of public recognition at times for some good things that have happened. As a leader, you often get some of that reflected glory. What I try to do, conscientiously, is to always make sure it's passed on to the appropriate people. If a newspaper wants to talk about an award, I'll say [they should] interview the teacher; that way they get their name in the paper rather than mine.

Drama was sometimes combined with celebration to make an event memorable in its link to the achievement of goals. Michael Barber dramatized success with fanfare.

I'm a big fan of America. There are lots of aspects of American culture I like. One is really celebrating success in a big way, which is so alien to Britain and to civil service. I used to get everybody and say they've done something and have everybody applaud them like they do in America. Sometimes we use music appropriate to the occasion, like the trumpet in Handel's *Messiah*. It's a brilliantly inspired bit of trumpet playing, so that was the one I picked for my last one.

Similarly, Rod Chamberlain understood the need for celebration, even though he admitted having to work against his nature to do so.

From my Germanic background we are used to working very hard . . . and then very hard . . . and then very hard. We seldom step back and say, "Let's have a party." This is something we do very well here [in Hawaii and in this school] . . . food and music and laughter. We have to learn how to maintain that as we grow larger.

The importance of diffusing stress was another priority for the community acclimation-minded leaders. As Helen Clark observed, "The jobs here are very demanding. I'm sensitive to the balance of family for those who work here."

The leaders were quite aware of the fact that all organizations are inevitably confronted with times of stress, as well as the lack of productivity and poor morale that such events can precipitate. Aware of the phenomenon, the leaders commonly described behavior that tuned them into the pulse of their organizations, either directly or indirectly. Nola Hambleton described her method for doing so.

> I rely on my assistant principals. I rely on them to be as helpful as they possibly can be to the teachers. I also rely on them to say, "Did you know that so-and-so is feeling really bad because something bad is happening in her life?" It's vital to have a tight team.

Similarly, Ian Fox worked to stayed tuned to his school environment.

> One of the things I try to do is monitor pressure points. When I can feel the levels increasing in the school, then I'll talk to my deputies and say, "Why don't we pull back?" So we'll have a staff meeting with food and drinks and just sit around and talk. I sometimes say to people, "Are you stressed, or are you busy? Because if you are stressed, that's really worrisome. If you are busy, how can we help you cope with that?" I think people can be busy without being stressed. I have to try to distinguish between the two. I monitor pressure points, pull back when necessary, and recognize the distinction between stress and business.

Boon Yoon Chiang made stress reduction a major priority in his corporations as a way to insure the free flow of ideas among diverse people.

> I try to develop a trusting and safe environment—giving employees a fair hearing for their ideas. You have to be sensitive about the various cultures, traditions, and customs of the people who work for you. I think some of the suggestions come because they feel that, because of their tradition or culture, that should be the way you should do things. I think you have to bear that in mind. That can be very useful because they do come up with something, sometimes, that the other people never thought about. We do encourage all employees to come up with ideas that may not be common to the others.

Deep concern for the well-being of his employees was evident in John Hood's observation that "I do very much care about the people with whom I work, and I care about them in a way that probably goes way beyond just the day-to-day activity of the office. . . . [Accordingly,] I ensure that things are balanced for them." John elaborated in adding that he regarded the failures of others as his own, that he put safety nets in place to allow others to aspire to the high standards he set, without fear of risk, blame, or recrimination if they came up short of total success.

In association with stress reduction and other contexts, the exercise of humor and play was often mentioned by the 36 leaders as essential elements within their repertoire of behaviors. Roger Harmon shared, "I go out to the volunteers and hang out with them and enjoy the people. I try to get some humor in play so the seriousness doesn't overwhelm them. I'm a better leader in the informal setting." Being nonthreatening and fun to be around was a self-described hallmark of Richard Bissen's style: "I try to create a conducive environment. I don't micro-manage, but every now and then I might have to say something. Everything I do is toward building opportunity. We will try everything we can [to help people be successful]." Patrick Sayne shared a similar sentiment in observing that the point was to "make people feel safe and not take yourself so seriously."

Many of the interviewed leaders saw humor as not only desirable, but essential. Working with at-risk students and very stressed teachers, Jeanne Dukes opined, "If you don't have a sense of humor, you won't be able to survive with these kids." Chet Bradley maintained that humor was indispensable.

> I use an awful lot of humor. To me, it's necessary to survive. I have to have a lot of humor in my life because it [often] isn't all that serious. Most people try to make it a hell of a lot more serious than it is. I try to use humor towards myself or someone I know . . . doing something to make that person laugh. Usually I try to direct it at myself and when people laugh, their [concern] has been diffused to some degree.

Julianne Lowe also used humor to diffuse difficult situations.

> I use humor with a degree of gentleness to reassure [people]. I let them know that their needs are very important to me and explain everything I possibly can. I also use humor to soften some of the sterner stuff. If you lose your cool or get ruffled easily, you're not going to make the grade.

Putting work into proper perspective was often seen as useful toward creating a supportive environment. Ian Fox spoke about creating the right balance between the seriousness of the organizational mission and a lighthearted approach to accomplishing it.

> If you go into our staff room, there is lots of laughter, banter, jokes, fun, but also serious stuff. I've always thought education is a serious issue, but you don't have to be serious doing it. We create a culture where teachers feel com-fortable about having a laugh, just by being relaxed when they are together and when they are with me.

MATCHING

Virtually all of the interviewed leaders commented on the importance of matchmaking, the business of acquiring and cultivating people who were both willing and able to contribute to the fulfillment of the organization's mission.

This performance area included making hard leadership decisions about moving or dismissing people in the best interest of both the organization and the individual.

Chet Bradley observed that matching committed and able people to specific purposes was a pillar of his leadership style.

> "I look for quirky and fun, not run-of-the-mill, people. Run-of-the-mill folks just won't last here."
>
> —*Jeanne Dukes*

> In any group, I first of all want to get to know the people. . . . I find something about them that I really think they can contribute to our overall goal. I try to find a niche for them and give them a chance.

Gary Rasmussen was in agreement with Chet's perspective. He approached matchmaking by "identifying skill sets for positions and really trying to get the best possible person to match that skill set." Beth Stevenson did this by "building a team of trusted people, committed to the same goals. . . . [Then,] if I know that someone is good at something that needs to be done, I offer that task to them." Michael Barber added to this insight in describing his unique opportunity to create a new division within his government, and to thereby judiciously match people to the challenging task at hand. He was highly aware of the importance of finding and putting in place the right people. "I transfer staff from previous jobs and otherwise try to find people that I can rely on. . . . I depend on supportive and dependable people."

For myriad reasons, when a necessary match didn't happen, the leaders were aware of their charge to do something about it. Bob Knight felt strongly that leaders have a responsibility to both avoid and resolve such mismatches.

> The worst thing is to force people into something that isn't a fit. Nobody goes into business to fail, and people don't come to work wanting to be the worst person they can be. My job is to put them in the right spot.

When a mismatch did occur, however, the interviewed leaders professed having the courage to make tough personnel decisions that furthered their vision and the greater purpose they served. Don Hazelwood discussed the matchmaking process within an orchestra.

> I take into consideration the value of one result against another, the personalities involved, and what they will lose or gain for themselves. If the decision doesn't go their way, then you can help them to handle the situation, even if it is not palatable. The good of the whole, the orchestra, is the standard. If we don't achieve the standard because players in key positions don't achieve a result, the orchestra and everyone will suffer. But you bend over backward to ease people through it in the most dignified manner.

Interestingly, school principal Ian Fox, likened his role to that of an orchestra leader.

> I feel I'm a conductor of orchestra. To me, that's what it is. I have some teachers here that others find a real pain, and in some ways, they are difficult, but they contribute very significantly to part of the school's strength. If they weren't doing that, maybe they would be a problem. I ask people what they want to do first, but also make sure that matches with what we are trying to do as a total school. It's a bit like the orchestra . . . you bring in the different players, and throughout the year, different people have different parts to play at different times. The philosophy we work to is [that] every one of us has responsibilities, and in small ways, we support other people. In return, we are supported in a very large way by the entire group.

CJ Nickerson shared that he aspired to hire people who had a strong work ethic, quick intelligence, and general compatibility with the mission of CHEF. Because of the personal relationships he nurtured within the organization, however, letting people go was the hard downside for him.

> I had to make a choice between what was in the best interest of the organization and its future growth and the best interest of this individual. When you know their story, there is pain in that kind of decision. It stays with you for a long time. In most cases, I try to ease the pain for them, but it doesn't necessarily ease the pain for me.

Gabor Halmai inherited serious staff mismatches when he assumed the role of President of the Soros Foundation in Hungary.

> Unfortunately, the budget was decreased by a quarter, and only 20 of the previous people working here remained. We had to start over with fund-raising, and there were no people left who were capable. . . . They were all educated, but none of them had ever worked with that problem before. The only real solution was to see what we needed—our real needs for the future—and find the right fit [of people] to meet those needs.

Delivering the bad news that a match was not apparent was often handled delicately, with both professional respect and personal empathy for the feelings of others. Rod Chamberlain commented on this important leadership responsibility.

> I try to talk to people individually. You confirm publicly and confront privately. A headmaster's job is to make people happy, and sometimes they would be happier someplace else. I once had a great tech person, but he did not have very good organizational skills. I eventually removed certain responsibilities from him. He came in the next day and said, "I want to thank you."

He later finished his doctorate and moved into university teaching, which matched his skills much better. Drucker said that a leader's responsibility is to maximize a person's strength and make their weaknesses irrelevant. That is a huge challenge. I look for the right skill set to fill the job, and if there isn't a match, I'm obligated to do something about it. I use open conversation and reflection to reach the right conclusion. Ultimately, the person will be happier in a place where there is a better match.

Rich Teerlink described the value of matching the right people with organizational values, as well as the importance of letting someone go because of a mismatch.

An interesting thing happened during one interview with a potential high-level executive with Harley. We went out to lunch, and he later reflected that all I talked about as Chairman and CEO were the values of the organization. He wondered why I didn't want to talk about him. But that wasn't my job. My job was to let him know that if you come to work for Harley, this is where we are coming from. People might get fired if they didn't fit with the values. That's an important thing to do in an organization, fire a high-level executive who doesn't live the values.

When fundamental values were not in conflict, Boon Yoon Chiang felt that Asian companies were better at dealing with mismatches than were American corporations.

I think the American way of looking at your employees is more like a digit. If you perform, you're all right. We are more humane and treat you like a human. You might, over a period of time, do very well, but you might not. We try to ship you around so that maybe if you don't do well in certain things, you might do better in other things. You can find what is best for you.

John Hood noted that his industry training in England promoted similar methods.

Ultimately, you are dealing with people's lives, their whole future. You must do everything in your power to help resettle them without causing damage to [the] institution, and in a sensitive manner. I feel a very deep responsibility to do that.

Strength of conviction and focus related to organizational purpose was clearly a driving criterion in determining good personnel matches. Jeanne Dukes indicated that this was very important. "The goal is to bring a diverse and talented group of people together who are committed to a common goal. If you don't have those characteristics, this isn't the place for you."

Frank Lukasavitz directly shared such wisdom with students at the Milwaukee Institute of Art and Design.

Do what you want to do. Find your niche and design what you like. If you are good at it, the money will come and you will live the good life forever after. [For example,] here were eight people who started this school from nothing. Are you willing to do the same?

EMPOWERING

The interviewed leaders expressed great faith in the abilities of the people they worked with. They described many approaches to empowering others with the skill and authority necessary for making meaningful contributions to the achievement of organizational goals. Beyond leadership behavior that acclimated and matched members to a community, there was a perceived need for cultivating confidence and capacity. Chet Bradley, for example, believed that leaders had to consciously make the effort to empower people to go do the job at hand.

> "Power dispersed is power multiplied."
>
> —*Patrick Sayne*

> It's reading them and then asking if they are comfortable doing it. If they need help, I give it. If they have questions, I try to answer them. Then I free them—give them the job—and get the hell out of their way.

Gary Rasmussen held a similar perspective. He maintained that once a person was appropriately matched to a position, it was important to "give them as much latitude as possible." Michael Barber joined the chorus in sharing that he lived by the mantra, "Find bright people and let them do their job."

Tim Brighouse extended the empowerment sentiment to the broad cultivation of leadership skill and disposition within an organization.

> I cannot lead long-term in one situation without speaking to and nurturing leadership values within the culture through careful appointments, inculcating leadership from within. . . . I start with what's good and then strive to spread it around.

Rich Teerlink described his approach to such empowerment in the business realm at Harley-Davidson.

> I have a willingness to give people an opportunity to design their own work. If we know we have to get something done, I'm not going to tell you how to do it. I'm not one to sit down and design the process. I'd rather have a conversation with the person who is going to do it. They might have a better idea than I would.

Rod Chamberlain shared similar sentiments on the theme of nurturing and freeing the capacity of others.

> I read a great story in high school called *Walden II* by B.F. Skinner about a utopia based on behaviorism. The guy who developed it [the utopian society] sat on the side of the hill and said, "Isn't it great to see what is done." I would like to be like that, to influence or nurture, and then step back and see that it continues to grow and that the core values are there. In any organization I have been in, the members have grown in capacity for impacting the community. Ultimately, I want to leave people better off and with the skills to do what they need to do.

Ulice Payne maintained that if a leader was serious about empowerment, it had to be equated to ownership. He asserted that the promotion of ownership for ideas and responsibilities was an essential means for growing leadership in others.

> You have to give up power and share it. If people take ownership in something, they will lead. It's the toughest thing, [ownership,] but when it is not there, it's only a job. It's like the difference between owning a house and renting. You will do the extra upkeep if it's yours.

The interviewed leaders were aware that the empowerment of others was also a means to making their own leadership responsibilities more manageable. Jeanne Dukes, for example, was very aware of her responsibility for facilitating the ongoing evaluation of organizational needs and priorities. Finding and empowering people to authoritatively act on those needs and priorities enabled her to maintain her attention to "the big picture." Nola Hambleton voiced a similar view in observing that entrusting important responsibilities to her competent deputy principals allowed her to work on larger issues and reach out to the community: "I don't do things that I know others can do just as well or better."

Rod Chamberlain was very cognizant of the leader's capacity for minimizing, as well as empowering, others. "To me, the power [of the leader] to inhibit or enhance is just so amazing. The power is implicit to condone or give blessing to certain things or to condemn something else."

Denese Henare shared Rod's sensitivity to the disempowerment of others. Her observation was that leaders must strive to "never take away the opportunity for others to make decisions themselves." Brenda Schoonover added her insight about the importance of balancing mundane delegation and meaningful empowerment.

> I think I am a very trusting leader. That goes back to being respectful. If you let people know you trust and respect them, but still set high standards and

goals, the average person will respond very effectively. It means that you are always in the state of trying to balance things. You are the boss, but you want to give people as much leeway as you can, to be independent, and to be teaching them skills. I think the challenge of leadership is achieving that delicate balance of giving people enough leeway so that they feel confident and develop, but also so that they know that you are in charge and that they respect you.

Providing quality feedback was frequently cited by the interviewed leaders as an important element of empowering others. The common sentiment was that feedback was a powerful tool for promoting self-analysis, and subsequently, a growing sense of self-efficacy. Accordingly, the leaders shared a variety of strategies for providing feedback as a means to empowerment. Margo Dévai described one method.

I provide positive feedback on what they do well and the help to correct mistakes after they have developed confidence. They are also asked to keep a written journal for self-assessment, and then I encourage them to come to me for help. I focus on the fact that everyone is able to improve. No one is perfect.

Rod Chamberlain shared another approach.

I try to listen to people and reflect back to them what they are trying to achieve and ask good questions. I also suggest they try things and then come back and tell me how it worked. I listen and feed back to them what they have said.

In some cases, feedback was part of a more formalized assessment system, as was the experience of Ian Fox.

In New Zealand, it is mandated that we have these appraisal policies, and what we have to do is heavily structured. What worries me is that in many schools, they work to a deficit model, trying to catch teachers out. So I have an appraisal policy where teachers are required to set four goals, related to teaching and learning, so that there is reflection. . . . It is a process of support. "How can I help you achieve your goals? What have you set for yourself? What about your team? Are there things that are needed in your team?"

Mandy Macleod used the need to evaluate staff as a means to encourage reflective thought.

I sit with each staff member, and we go over their goals. I ask for any ways that they feel I can support them in fulfilling their goals. I look at ways that they are working toward these goals and try to encourage them. I also encourage them to self-evaluate.

Rich Teerlink had a critical view of the merits of the traditional performance evaluation process versus what could be.

> We don't have quality conversations in [most] organizations. Instead, we have evaluation every quarter. Set up the half-hour meetings and tell people what they do wrong. Why don't we ask people what objectives they would set for themselves? Those [are the] conversations that build trust.

The leaders' bottom line about feedback appeared to be that it might be hard work, but it was worth it. Ulice Payne observed that "leadership is helping people do what they think they can't. It's about unleashing their energy." Given that perception, a leader, such as Leotis Watson, would be disposed to go the extra feedback mile.

> I believe in the Montessori way—I give you every opportunity to learn in your own way and at your own pace. I will give you all the materials you need. I will give you all the feedback you need. If an associate has made a bad decision, I'm not going to write him up. We are just going to talk about it, so it won't happen again. And if it's two wrongs, we are going to talk about it again. Then if a third happens, I'm still not going to write you up, but I will try to show you that we value you as an associate . . . [and] that we are here to be of service.

TEAMING

The community-building reflections of 36 leaders also revealed that they often facilitated collaborative relationships as means to effect the achievement of organizational goals. This behavior pattern conveyed an intuitive leadership sense for what Beth Stevenson termed "changing the quality of connections between people." Roger Harmon, for example, was very clear about his interest in promoting collaboration as Director of Peace Corps Thailand.

> "We are all part of a team, we are all kings. And when one advances, we all advance."
>
> —Leotis Watson

> I emphasize teamwork. Maybe that's my own personal style. I feel comfortable with that. I think it is what is needed right now in Peace Corps Thailand. I see so many capable people able to go off and do their narrow job, and the right hand doesn't know what the left hand is doing. I've worked very hard to meet with everyone on a regular basis. We are building an intraculture, a special kind of [connected] culture.

Michael Barber structured a coalition of 25 people into flexible and interactive work teams to facilitate synergy and action.

It was never just me. We formed a guiding coalition that I could absolutely rely on. We went through some really hard times on school closures, but the guiding coalition would never break. . . . The Delivery Unit is very small . . . [but] we can work together, the 25 of us. I spend a lot more time with people than in my previous job. I actually think about each of [the team members] individually now. We've basically done away with hierarchy, which is another part of the government culture we're trying to change. People are in flexible teams. They like that; they find it challenging and they helped me invent it. We're much more collaborative, so we invent our systems together and we try things out.

Alex Banful promoted both spontaneous and deliberate interactions between people in his organization.

We hold a lot of informal meetings in the corridor. It starts with one person, two, and before you can say jack, we have the complete strategic meeting going on in the corridor. No one works in isolation here. My approach is like soccer, where you have 11 players. We discourage competitiveness internally, so we move in to solve problems across teams. As team manager, I reserve the right to switch players around any way that is needed to get the energy of different perspectives.

In her school setting, Mandy Macleod worked hard to develop teamwork, even when doing so was not popular with everyone.

I just don't talk the talk, I walk the walk on team building. Everything in the middle school is done in teams. There is a facilitator, and everyone gets to say their say and everyone's voice is heard, [and] we have essential agreements that everyone agrees to respect. Some people went into team building screaming and kicking. But I'm really convinced. I think that people need to have their voices heard.

Brenda Schoonover found that team formation was essential to managing and surviving the complexities of her leadership challenges.

I think Togo [where she was Ambassador] was probably the place where I had the biggest challenge with morale. I followed a really dynamic ambassador, a hard act to follow. We had power outages, a presidential election that was not very satisfactory, and civil unrest. Late one Sunday morning, the staff called me about 7 A.M. and said, "Madam, there's [a] problem. . . . There's gunfire." We evacuated everyone on Embassy staff to my house. I had about 40 people at my house. . . . In the course of that day, we had weathered all of those things . . . and we became a team.

Team formation occurred, of course, under far less dramatic circumstances as well. Patrick Sayne described his low-key approach to promoting a synergetic culture.

Humor can develop camaraderie. It also eases the way for idea sharing, where everyone's opinion is valued. That doesn't mean that all opinions are of equal value. If your opinion doesn't meet with universal approbation, that doesn't mean that you shouldn't share it. You [as the leader] have to provide an environment that allows for risking and an environment for listening. I do this by never using or allowing serious put-downs and by acknowledging comments with consideration of the ideas offered. There is something to be said for the usual social graces . . . to be polite and listen. But it has to be authentic and honest . . . not game playing.

As someone who shared considerable responsibility for a dramatic turnaround in the fortunes of his company, Rich Teerlink understood the strategic use of teams as a primary means for achieving the organization's mission.

Our business process at Harley was to capture within every employee the ability to answer four questions: How should we behave? What's important? Who do we serve? and How will we know success? The purpose was to communicate what individuals needed to know to achieve the mission, objectives, and strategies. My work group should be clear about the organization's strategy and working to move it forward. If I look at what my work group's job is, then I should be able to define my job pretty well and work toward making that happen. And knowing that if I make it happen, my work group will make it happen, and [in this fashion] the strategy goes right through the organization. And we have a success.

Centering

In close association with their description of a strong orientation toward community building, the interviewed leaders further observed a propensity for behaviors that centered self and associates on what was most worthy of attention and effort. Such centering behavior was consistent with the leaders' sense of their passionate character. They were driven by their passions to build and serve a viable community capable of achieving a compelling purpose. Beyond building the community, moreover, there was

> "It is my job to sell a set of attitudes."
>
> —Mechai Viraviadya

a perceived need for acting in a manner that maintained focus. Thus, the leaders described how they acted to center their organizations through behaviors that included *dialoguing* and *modeling*.

DIALOGUING

In the eyes of most of the interviewed leaders, centering self and others on what was most important necessarily began with accessibility and healthy dialogue within their community. To that end, the leaders expressed a particular interest in having others feel comfortable in approaching them with ideas, problems, and challenges—both the good and bad news. Helen Clark, for example, talked about taking the arrogance out of the role of Prime Minister. "I am the least pompous and the most accessible Prime Minister New Zealand has ever had. Three decades in politics before becoming Prime Minister keeps me down to earth." To sustain this perspective, Helen maintained her old office in the neighborhood of Auckland that originally elected her to parliament, a location in which constituents could easily access her and her staff on a regular basis.

> "I am approachable and unobtrusive."
>
> — Ross Gilbert

In an educational setting, Mandy Macleod described how she maintained accessibility for anyone who wanted to interact with her during the hectic school day.

> I have an open door policy. People feel completely at ease to come in. I think that is really important. They feel that they can come and speak to me at any time, and I will always make time if it is at all possible.

Mandy engaged her faculty early on with this open attitude and, as a result, she developed a set of norms to live by as a leader.

> When I came to this school, I asked the staff for their expectations of their principal. We boiled it down to these seven:
>
> 1. Be visible.
> 2. Provide clear strong direction and caring leadership.
> 3. Support teachers.
> 4. Communicate honestly, fairly and personally.
> 5. Establish consensus.
> 6. Encourage professional growth.
> 7. Respect and recognize achievements and maintain a sense of humor.

As superintendent of a large urban school district, Tim Brighouse advocated for openness as a means to "talk, listen, and make time for others." He routinely invited people out to dinner for open conversation about the critical issues facing his large urban school district. For Ulice Payne, such dialoguing was essential to his leadership.

> I have to know who I am leading. It's getting to know them [through] talking, but mainly [through] listening. Most people don't listen enough. As someone in a management position with the Brewers, people wanted to tell me what

they thought. You have to ask them what they want, listen, and then turn around and give them what they want . . . if you can.

Direct and honest communication was thought to be important within open dialogue, even if it meant dealing with uncomfortable situations. Fanny Law described her value for such honesty.

I'm a person who is very forthright. I just speak the truth, which gets me into trouble sometimes. Last year was supposed to be a bad year for me in terms of Chinese superstitions, and I did get into a lot of controversies. I sometimes reappraise whether I should be a politician. I want to be able to speak truth to authority, and as a minister, that is sometimes difficult to do.

Christine Rodriguez maintained that an honest and forthright manner was the only moral option when dialoguing with others, a position echoed by Richard Bissen's uncompromising "I believe in the power of truth." As Don Hazelwood observed, however, open dialogue is sometimes a sensitive and delicate matter.

I think you have to say the thing as you see it yourself. You've got to be diplomatic, but you have to couch it in terms that also provide an opening for the person to avoid total embarrassment. You can't cut off one's possibility of retreating from a situation. You can't cut off a person's dignity. A person has to be approached if they are not reaching a particular standard in whatever they are doing. They [also] have to be allowed an opportunity to retreat from the situation in the most dignified manner that they can; otherwise, you are doing more damage than good.

Bob Knight proposed that forthright communication was a behavior to be modeled and encouraged.

You have to pay attention to rumors and interpretations. I listen to what they say and then try to clear up misunderstandings. I pay attention and try to clarify what is going on. Say it clear, and don't beat around the bush. Say why you are thinking it. I try to teach everyone to just say it and not be afraid.

Within open and ongoing dialogue, the interviewed leaders also perceived opportunity to wield the power of story in the form of a consistent and meaningful message. For example, to maintain the focus of his work within national interests, Kuami Pianim constantly took the message of joint responsibility to his countrymen.

It's very important that we all try to lift our society up. As a leader, you can never get too far away from the society and the people. If you do, you may look behind and see that no one is following you. You have to articulate the principles you believe in . . . get them out in ways that all can understand.

Mechai Viraviadya not only understood the power of story but also his place in it.

> One of the things I've learned is to see the step I'm about to take or recommend in the context of history. I can think how this looks as a possible narrative in history. It's the equivalent in time to seeing the countryside from a balloon in space. You can see your decision as history will perceive it. I try to get people to think like that.

Brenda Schoonover commented on the importance of constructing a shared story of understanding through dialogue.

> One of our challenges after September 11th is telling America's story. Because you get this "Why do they hate us so much? Why do they misunderstand us so much?" I think the other side of that is telling America what other people think of us and how we should handle that as well.

Skill in dialoguing and telling the story of the organization or a particular issue was important to Ulice Payne, as instilled in him by his college professors.

> People who can't communicate can't lead. You have to know your subject and know your audience. It's real simple. Don't talk about something you don't know, and make sure you know who you're talking to. Unless I can get to your level of experience, interest, and taste and really know my subject, then I can't communicate with you. Without that, people don't understand where you are leading or why.

Working toward a clear understanding of vision and goals was seen as the ultimate purpose of dialoguing with and within the organization. Rod Chamberlain often employed questions within his interactions with others as a means to clarify and refocus organizational purpose.

> Who are we here to serve and how do we make that happen? I think it is interesting how often we forget that. We are here to serve the children and their families. The employees forget that sometimes, and it is my job to keep bringing it up. My style is let's try to be clear about what needs to be done and by when and then to keep putting that out on the table.

Rod further elaborated on his efforts to orient and advance organizational purpose in stating, "I characterize my leadership as trying to build a consensus vision, breaking that down into the next steps of what we need to do and a timeline for getting it done." Ian Fox also worked to make sure his staff was clear about timelines and priorities.

> We have an advance schedule of what our meeting topics are, and they should all fit in with our school goals for the year. Teachers know that they have some

responsibility in each area, and there's a leader for that group. My responsibility is to try and work with the groups. "How can I help you?" To a degree, that's what I think my job is, [that is,] to make the teacher's job easier and to allow the teachers to do their work more efficiently and effectively.

Some of the leaders had walked into organizations where clarity about purpose had not been well established. Roger Harmon shared such an experience.

When I came here, I felt there was confusion about where we were headed in the program, and people were leaving because they didn't know and [because] policies were unclear. The important thing is to clarify the goals of the organization, to make it clear what we understand the job to be. I emphasize the opportunity for defining secondary efforts within the project and also personal goals: "Why are you here? What brought you here?" and "How can we support that?"

Whatever their circumstances and experiences, the interviewed leaders expressed a shared value for leadership that promoted dialogue that helped clarify purpose and processes and thereby better center the efforts of the organization. Beth Stevenson captured the essence of this view.

One of my goals is to facilitate really open communication and goal clarity, role clarity, what we want to accomplish . . . helping others get the mission and feel passionate about it, connected to [it], and finding out what they want to accomplish too.

Furthermore, dialoguing behavior was perceived by the interviewed leaders as important, but not sufficient to their centering responsibilities. Indeed, most of the leaders believed that a crucial part of their role was to advocate aggressively for their values, that is, to sell their ideas and generate like passion in others.

For a politician such as Helen Clark, advocating for ideas and positions was somewhat expected behavior. Helen shared, however, about how hard she worked to set the media agenda each week in order to advocate for her message. "It's so easy to get distracted. We plan the agenda for the week and then feed the press information at the beginning of each week. I am routinely on television programs, getting our message out."

Rich Teerlink shared how he aggressively advocated for the codification of core values for his manufacturing company: "Tell the truth, be fair, keep promises, and respect the individual and intellectual curiosity." Not surprisingly, Rich easily traced the company values to beliefs and values forged during his formative years. "These values resonate with me on a personal level—mother with her golden rule and my dad respecting all the people in the factory."

MODELING

The interviewed leaders shared how they valued and engaged in dialogue as a means to continuously center organizational sense of purpose and process. Simply put, the leaders believed that it was productive to conduct an ongoing conversation with their associates about what was important to do and how to best do it. Beyond talking about what was important, however, they were also prone to walk their talk. In fact, the interviewed leaders collectively observed that they did not have the right—nor did they believe it to be an effective leadership strategy—to ask others to do work or adopt behaviors that they weren't willing to take on themselves. Chet Bradley addressed this perspective:

> "I would never ask anyone to do something that I wouldn't do myself. Leading by example is the key."
>
> —Richard Bissen

> My style of leadership is that I don't expect others to do something that I wouldn't do. . . . I also know that I can't do it all, so I try to figure out what I can best do within the system to model what is important and valued.

Some such form of modeling was seen as an important strategy by most of the leaders. Gavan Flick mentored young Aboriginal artists and tried to model necessary approaches to success in modern Australian society.

> We have Aboriginal artists come into the gallery. We tell them it's going to be tough, and then by advice and example, we show them how they can stick it out. I think it is important to deal with the one, so we can educate the ten.

Margo Dévai described how she used modeling in her work with teachers: " I am very good at working with others, patient and understanding. . . . I do a lot of role modeling to show teachers how to build positive relationships with their students." Boon Yoon Chiang described the application of a similar approach in a corporate setting.

> One of the things I try to do is make myself a role model. I could describe it as leading by example. Unlike some people, who tend to be somewhat aloof to subordinates, I tend to adopt an open-door approach so that people can come anytime and see me. I go around and observe the various operations, not only to see those in charge, but to interact with all the people working in the company. I want to see and engage the problems they have, what they are doing. Sometimes they even tell me their personal problems. Interpersonal relationships are very important.

When nonproductive behaviors surfaced in their organization, modeling was often cited by the leaders as the means they used to demonstrate a more productive way of behaving. John Hood found the need to do so early in his administration experience at the university:

> I consistently try to be a role model, to set standards through osmosis. The classic example is e-mail protocol. I was so angry when I first arrived and saw the way that some of my colleagues addressed others in e-mail, with no natural courtesy. I have religiously used a standard protocol in terms of the way I address people, sign off, and the way I address things in the middle. Most people have actually picked up on that, and we've seen an improvement.

Authenticity in what was modeled was paramount to the integrity of the behavior. Bob Knight felt that credibility was built by authentic behavior. "I lead by example. I can do pretty much what everyone does here, so that builds credibility." Denese Henare expressed a similar view. "There is power in positive example, but you have to live it from within." Leotis Watson also acknowledged the power of example.

> To me, the key is consistency. They see it and hear it day in and day out. I am trying to perfect a way in myself that through a performance on a consistent basis, they see this guy is doing the same thing every day in every way.

Mandy Macleod concurred that it was important to model action aligned to purpose. "You not only have to be visionary, but you have to be seen doing it."

Thinking

In addition to describing prominent performance behaviors in the fields of community building and centering purpose, the interviewed leaders revealed a propensity for engaging self and others in productive thinking. Having previously described themselves as contemplative in character, they observed that they also acted to exercise and stretch other brains. When it came to thinking, the 36 leaders were of a mind that what was good for the goose was also good for the geese. To that end, the leaders shared how they *informed* and *challenged* thinking within the performance of their leadership roles.

> "Good leaders speculate, ask the right questions, and get people to think about what might be . . . without giving the answers."
>
> —Tim Brighouse

INFORMING

The interviewed leaders believed in giving their associates ample food for thought. They did so by facilitating the flow of information through their

> "I love learning and connecting ideas to people. My job is to create synapses all over the place."
>
> —*Jeanne Dukes*

organizations. This behavior was prompted in part by the belief that it is just good leadership practice to do so. John Hood, for example, was clear about the necessity of open communication.

> Open communication is very important to me. I don't think you can afford anything other than very open leadership in any organizational setting. There are no secrets. I communicate totally and openly about anything except what is confidential. Open leadership, no secrets.

Similarly, Gary Rasmussen viewed the sharing of information as a leadership imperative.

> I think you have to be really transparent and be able to explain and reveal information that shows the way you operate. People can see that as a natural thing; you don't have to prove it every time.

Richard Bissen, however, zeroed in on the fundamental reason for sharing information in stating, "I provide the information that is needed to make good decisions." Ross Gilbert provided an example of this approach in describing why and how he structured data so that it was easily digestible and usable.

> I believe reflection without data is useless. I do a summary report on student evaluations and post it on the Web. We are the most open place in the university. . . . We get rave reviews for the quality of it. We talk about teaching and openly discuss it.

Many of the leaders referenced research as an information source that they disseminated to associates. As someone in charge of policy analysis and administration, Michael Barber, for one, relied heavily on sharing current research. "I started implementing things using the research on policy design and implementation. It turns out the research was right. If you do these things, others will learn how to do it."

As a practitioner, Tim Brighouse looked at research information in relationship to life on the frontline. "We are continuously learning from practice, and we go beyond the edge of research to practical implementation." Other leaders supported information flows across the organization by bridging employees to employees. Jeanne Dukes described the phenomenon this way: "I facilitate the connections between people and other people and people and programs, [and] we do a huge amount of learning. I encourage teachers to get involved in an interest area and then share with others."

In addition to the above observations, virtually all of the community-building leadership behaviors described earlier in this chapter—particularly those directed at acclimating, empowering, and teaming—served to advance and enrich the flow of information within. This is an important point. If the leaders were not this attentive to richly informing the minds of their associates, they would necessarily realize less return from their efforts to challenge and stretch those same minds.

CHALLENGING

The interviewed leaders professed personal value for contemplative reflection. Their interview responses also revealed that they challenged others to the exercise of conscious reflection. That is, reflective thinking was not viewed as of value only to self, but also as an attribute to foster in others.

> "You have to get off the conveyor belt going at 100 miles an hour to be able to stand back and reflect."
>
> —Denese Henere

The 36 leaders shared numerous stories about how they challenged the thinking of associates by simply structuring the time, place, and purpose that invites the phenomenon to occur. Brenda Schoonover provided one such account of a simple meeting structure.

> About three weeks ago, I had a meeting at the house about "spring cleaning." I had the political, economic, public affairs, administration, and defense over for a session. The idea was not so much to talk about substance, but to evaluate how we do things and how we can do them better. From there, we came up with a list of recommendations.

Likewise, Ross Gilbert talked about being credited with holding the most effective and reflective, yet uncomplicated, committee meetings in the conservatory: "I collect and organize data for use in self and departmental reflection in a safe atmosphere of 'what can we learn from this to improve.'"

Beyond basic meeting frameworks, Nola Hambleton supported other structures to better ensure effective interchanges of information and ideas.

> Quality circles involve a group of people—which can be fixed or constantly changing in composition—that take a topic and use all of the information that everyone has read about to exchange ideas, to be stimulated, to improve something. I try to encourage creativity [through this process].

Other leaders attempted to embed and habituate reflection into daily routines. Michael Barber observed that "the real task is asking each of them [staff] to reflect each day on what they've learned, because each day will bring a phenomenal learning experience. We're trying to get back to a learning organization culture." Jeanne Dukes felt so strongly about the power of reflection that she mandated a structure to encourage it.

We require that every school site [engage in] decompressing at the end of each day, at least an hour and a half. It can be preparation time, but turns into bitch time. "What did you do? Did you try this?" And then they laugh and plan for the next day. We build in time for the whole staff to get together. They don't want to do it, but I really think it is important for them to know each other and know that they can rely on each other.

Realizing the confines of the organization may work against reflection, a number of the leaders supported off-site opportunities. Boon Yoon Chiang described such a policy he initiated within his company.

From time to time, we send our top-level people for a short course and [otherwise] enable them to reflect on what they have been doing and whether they need to change things they are doing or make it more effective.

Within the confines of an educator's day, Mandy Macleod found ways to promote similar reflection on a smaller scale.

In the school day, time to reflect is almost impossible. I encourage people to take "down time" for themselves, to look to their own physical and psychological well-being. I say, "If you have a free period, go and have a cup of coffee off the premises."

The legacy of John Hood's Socratic education came to bear in the way he engaged reflective thinking in his employees.

I tend to pose questions and, as much as possible, leave people to reflect on them and respond to them as they will. I do this both formally in meetings and informally. I may take a couple of minutes to chat out on the sidewalk, constantly challenging them to think.

Rich Teerlink used four questions to structure reflection about the purpose of the business: (a) What's important? (b) Who do we serve? (c) How should we behave? and (d) How will we know success? He added that if you make people aware and provide information in a loose structure, "they will create alignment with purpose."

Donald Gwira had a very systematic process for reflecting on how to best achieve goals, a process he shared with associates in his organization.

I do a mental analysis; it takes A, B, C, D, and E to get to where we want to go. Then I look back and retrace my steps. Nine times out of ten, you will not end up where you started out. If you are able to retrace your steps, then you know you're on the right track. When you're looking backward, you see all the things you didn't see by thinking forward. This probably came from my martial arts training where I learned to do *katas*, a series of movements that prepares one to defend against several attackers. With most *katas*, one begins and ends at the same spot. I've used that [same] process mentally, and it has worked for me.

Many of the interviewed leaders described a tolerance for ambiguity and taking time to think things through. Such tolerance figured into how they challenged themselves and others to think more productively. They purposefully fostered "wait time" within important decisions, promoting reflection on the means as well as the ultimate outcome. John Hood commented on the importance of this tolerance for "staying gray."

> I learned from Steve Simple at USC, who had a nice way of staying gray about things, hearing the different points of view and not making a decision about something until you have clarity. So I do spend a lot of time talking and listening informally.

Similarly, in working to create a culture of reflection, CJ Nickerson described gathering his staff in a neutral setting and conducting an analysis of something that might not have worked well in the organization.

> I always try to put our mistakes in the context of "What can we learn from this?" We just want to hear what we have to say, not for evaluation but for clarification and so that we can explore some other options. If we reached a conclusion, I would insist that we sit on it for a couple of days to let it cook, to see if any other ideas surfaced and test our comfort level with any preliminary decision we might have reached.

Revelations about the leaders' contemplative character, as presented earlier in this chapter, similarly described behavior aligned to not rushing to judgment and allowing time for reflection before making a decision. John Hood was able to place that personal behavior in an organizational context that valued the "fermentation" of ideas.

> One does it quietly by walking around the organization, talking to colleagues about ideas and getting their reaction. For an organization to work, the organization has to have a consciousness about the things we should be pursuing. You have to have an organizational patience to let things simmer.

At the top end of their propensity for challenging the thinking of self and others, the interviewed leaders promoted deeper analysis and creativity. Reflecting a fundamental belief in the power of individuals to "figure it out for themselves," the leaders advocated encouraging others to dig deeper and speculate about alternative possibilities. To that end, Frank Lukasavitz would admonish his students, "Don't think of 1 way, think of 20 ways," and Mandy Macleod would routinely "let people work on solving their own problems." Given, however, that leaders are often expected to provide "the" answer, delaying closure about an issue was noted as an exercise in leadership restraint. Rod Chamberlain frequently engaged people in conversation that helped them to think about their lives and what they wanted to accomplish, resisting any temptation to tell them what he thought was best. "I was recently sitting down with one of our custodians and asked 'where are you going, and what are you doing to get there?' Being clear on what you want to be and persevering is what it's about."

Challenging the thought processes of others was not without its risks. The interviewed leaders were aware of the need to be open to unintended results. John Hood found that to be the case in the world of academia.

> The university is full of extraordinarily talented individuals, but very eccentric as well, and one has to be sure that the culture allows those sorts of people to thrive. And occasionally one gets surprises, and you sort of stand back and think about what does the surprise do in the context of what the institution is, . . . and accept it. I'm very fortunate to come from a corporate background where the power of ideas was a core value, and I think that's a core value of mine too. The power of ideas should be on the floor at all times.

It was also observed that different individuals are more or less accustomed to the exercise of reflective thinking. Accordingly, in some instances, a leader who valued reflection would necessarily encourage and challenge such thinking. CJ Nickerson, for example, hired someone for a trial period on the advice of others and for months heard only textbook answers to his questions.

> Finally one day I got in his face and said, "Larry, if I want to know what Dr. So-and-So says, I will ask them, but I am asking you for your opinion. What do you think?" The next day, he gave me his opinion and never stopped. Sixteen years later, he replaced me as President of CHEF.

Personally prone to exploring options and seeking alternatives, the leaders also described how they helped people to see problems from different perspectives. Gary Rasmussen shared one such everyday example.

> We just had an incident with the principal being very upset to find out that he is not getting as big a playground because of the covered walkway and planter. My architect supervisor is saying that the kids have this big covered walkway to do activities. There are two different perspectives here. When the architect is upset, I say, "Leslie this is how Bruce sees it," and vice versa to Bruce. I try to help them put themselves in the other's perspective.

Michael Barber encouraged discourse as a means to bring forth issues, examine alternatives, and generate viable solutions.

I deal with four sectors of state: health, the home office, education, and transport, and there's a secretary of state for each of those. I show what progress had been made every two months. My job is to report on progress against plan and against the data trajectory. Obviously, not everything goes perfectly because this is the real world, so when something goes wrong, we help the relevant department design a solution, and we do the problem solving with them.

In a school context, Nola Hambleton observed a similar need for reflective discourse.

I am constantly looking for new ideas at this school. I've got a vision of raising the standards and making this a place for children to come where they not only enjoy their environment, but they know what they are going to learn and learn it as well. Talking and discussing ways to do this [as a staff] is important.

Lessons Learned

Human beings enjoy a capacity for consciously deciding how to behave in given circumstances. Such reflection is always influenced, nevertheless, by value orientations to the quality of our existence. In this fashion, attributes of individual character, particularly our motivating moral principles, influence how we behave.

Leaders make hundreds, perhaps thousands, of decisions every day about how to conduct themselves while interacting with others within diverse contexts. From that experience reference, the 36 interviewed leaders were very cognizant of the influence of character on their behavior. Indeed, they described their leadership behavior as character in action. Richard Bissen, who saw himself as trustworthy, spoke of modeling trusting behaviors so that others would follow suit. Beth Stevenson, who saw herself as empathetic, described how she put a great deal of energy into building a community of support where all employees would feel safe, understood, and valued. Those were but two examples of how the interviewed leaders perceived a performance path that traveled from values to character to behavior. *Values inspired the leadership character that was acted out as leadership behavior.* Accordingly, the leaders' described behavior was markedly congruent with their core values (see Figure 6.1). Their observations about leadership behavior also resonated with a long history of research interest in "universal effective leader behavior" (Ayman, 2004, p. 150).

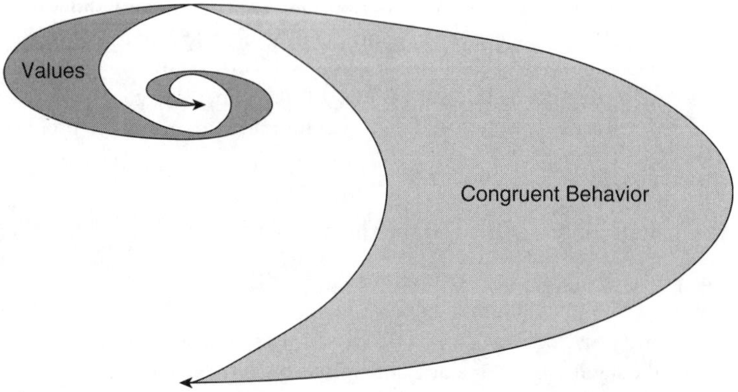

Congruent behavior both reflects and reinforces core values within a coherent relationship between leadership formation and performance.

Examples of Core Values

Human Dignity
Hard Work
High Standards
Competence
Productive Thinking
Service to Others
Making a Difference

Examples of Congruent Behavior

Community Building
Centering
Thinking

Figure 6.1   Coherent Leadership Is Extended and Reinforced by Congruent
Behavior

Further Conversation

The reflections presented in this chapter describe how the leadership performance of 36 leaders was acted out across three prominent fields of behavior. Exercise 6.1 invites you to rejoin the conversation at this point to examine how your leadership behavior is acted out. (Again, this is a reflection exercise that you can complete alone or through conversation with colleagues, as you prefer.)

EXERCISE 6.1   Further Conversation: Fields of Behavior

With reference to your prior reflections in Further Conversation Exercise 2.1 and Further Conversation Exercise 5.1:

A. What are the core values that orient your approach to life and leadership?

B. What character traits define your leadership?

C. How are your leadership character traits congruent with your core values?

D. What does your leadership look like (i.e., your defining leadership behavior)?

E. How is your leadership behavior congruent with your core values?

F. Why might congruency in leadership values, character, and behavior matter?

G. Why might community building be a valuable field of leadership behavior?

H. Why might centering purpose be a valuable field of leadership behavior?

I. Why might informing and challenging thinking be a valuable field of leadership behavior?

J. What is the most important field of behavior for a leader to engage in? Why?

7

Capacity Connected

Look at the world around you. It may look like an immovable, implacable place. It is not. With just the right push—in just the right place—it can be tipped.

—Gladwell (2000, p. 259)

Performed Toward Key Connections

Leadership is a process of influencing others toward the achievement of goals. In Part One (Chapters 1–3), 36 leaders described their leadership formation. Those accounts portrayed leaders who were shaped, called, committed, and compelled to influence others toward the achievement of goals. Thus far in Part Two of this narrative (Chapters 4–6), the leaders have described how they performed as leaders—how they acted to influence others toward the achievement of goals. Within this description of how they conducted their leadership business, a picture emerges of value-aligned performance as defined by force of character (e.g., humble, passionate, contemplative) across prominent fields of behavior (e.g., community building, centering, thinking). As the leaders described it, what they did (i.e., their behavior) emerged from who they were (i.e., their character) as dictated by what they believed to be important (their values).

There is further insight to be realized, however, within this group reflection about leadership performance. If we step back from the intimate portrayal of congruency between leadership values, character, and behavior, a "big picture" of leadership influence emerges. The leaders' reflections about the alignment of values, character, and behavior begin to reveal the essence of their performance—how they forged influential relationships with other people. Specifically, this more comprehensive view brings into focus prominent leadership connections to the social, emotional, and reflective dimensions of human capacity for growth and achievement.

A Social Connection

When asked to describe the character of their leadership behavior, 36 exemplary leaders from diverse contexts across the globe immediately shared perceptions and anecdotes that defined their social acuity and disposition. They were very attuned to the importance of their relationships with others. This might be expected, given the implied social foundation of the leadership phenomenon. If leadership is a process of influencing others toward the achievement of goals, an obvious key element within that definition is the dynamic between a leader and "others." A strong social orientation to leadership performance was also to be expected, given the leaders' espoused values and commitments (e.g., value for human dignity, equality and diversity, service to others, and making a difference in the world). The 36 leaders' intuitive sense of a leadership connection to the social nature of human capacity was, nonetheless, impressive.

MEANT FOR EACH OTHER

Human capacity for learning and achieving goals is very social in nature. Born of rich social experience over millions of years, humankind is endowed with hypersocial instincts—natural and powerful abilities for memory, language, empathy, sympathy, collaboration, and reasoning. Indeed, our social bias is such that it is socially expectant, dependent, extended, and oriented to virtue.

The unfolding of our capacity for learning and achievement is expectant of the same social experience that constructed it over evolutionary time. Social experience, moreover, is the great provocateur of the quality of thinking and learning that we depend on to realize our potential. To satisfy this overarching need and disposition for interaction in a society of minds, we have invented a variety of media that extend social interaction beyond face-to-face encounters (e.g., art, writing, print, telephone, radio, film, television, and the Internet). We also have an instinctive social sense of virtue as demonstrated by our moral orientation to prosocial behavior.

SUBJECT TO LEADERSHIP INFLUENCE

We have an overarching human need to connect with others and to create the networks of relationships and communities of the mind that help us solve problems, make good decisions, and create better systems and technologies. If we appreciate that human capacity leans on interpersonal relationships, it is then at least somewhat apparent that leaders might seek to nurture such relationships toward the achievement of goals. They would behave in ways that would favorably influence the quality of relationships within the members of a group committed to a particular purpose, as well as relationships between self and others.

As it happened, the 36 interviewed leaders were very aware of the importance of social relationships. Again, such an orientation might be expected, given the social dynamic of leadership as a process of influencing others toward the achievement of goals. The leaders' attention to the social nature of human capacity was, nevertheless, rich and profound. By their accounts, the nurture of social relationships was a leadership priority. It was a priority, notably, that was served by character and behavior that connected to social instinct, expectation, dependency, and virtue orientation in real contexts.

The leaders' connections to social capacity can be observed being played out in the form of humble, passionate, and contemplative character aligned to community building, centering, and inquiring behavior. Through such force of leadership character across prominent fields of leadership behavior, the leaders portrayed their propensity for facilitating meetings of minds, cultivating common purpose, and extending the mind's reach. Whether they did so as a result of intuition or formal study and conscious reflection matters not.

The leaders advanced social connections to and between others by being respectful, empathetic, and trustworthy. Such connections were furthered by purposeful attention to acclimation, matching, empowerment, and teaming. A compelling sense of shared purpose was cultivated by passionate focus and straightforward dialogue and example. The leaders were also markedly attentive to informing and challenging the minds of others toward the accomplishment of a shared vision.

Ultimately, the leaders' reflections about performance character and behavior revealed a strong instinct for social relationships that advanced the capacity for achieving compelling and mutually held goals.

An Emotional Connection

Suffice it to say that the 36 interviewed leaders were very much in touch with their own emotions, as well as the emotions of those they aspired to influence. A wide range of emotions richly accented their interview reflections. Joy, anger, amusement, sorrow, and a host of other emotional states flared across the leaders' reflections about how they performed toward the advancement of their leadership purpose. They were acutely aware of the emotional leadership energy generated by their core values. Their accounts of being disposed toward passionate character and centering behavior also defined their leadership performance as emotionally fueled and connected.

MOVED BY THE MOMENT

It's hard to deny our emotional nature. Who hasn't felt the joy of friendship or love, the anger of conflict, or the sadness of loss? The human brain is awash in emotion, and the proof is in our behavior. Each of us can recall multiple experiences of being happy, sad, angry, or disgusted and acting accordingly. As a matter of fact, it would be more difficult to recall a time when you felt no emotion whatsoever. This is because emotion is hardwired into our system as a survival mechanism. Emotion is the means by which we quickly screen, judge, and react to a vast array of environmental information. We are wired to act reflexively first and reflectively afterwards.

Emotion is what moves us to attention, judgment, motivation, and reasoned management of mind-body states. It involves neural and glandular systems that trigger changes in mind and body in response to evaluations of external and internal information—reflexive changes that arouse attention to what is important. Classic examples of emotion-triggered mind-body states are fear, anger, joy, sorrow, surprise, and disgust. Reflexive arousal systems associated with emotions initiate our immediate and automatic responses to environmental stimulation (e.g., fight or flight). Subsequently, emotional centers interact with rational reasoning systems in our brain to judge the merits of events and available options.

Emotion also plays a role in motivation by both arousing and sustaining passion about things that matter. Furthermore, emotion represents a brain-body function that is manageable, but only after the fact. We are able to recognize and mediate emotional responses after they occur; this is a capacity referred to as emotional intelligence.

SUBJECT TO LEADERSHIP INFLUENCE

The interviewed leaders observed that they were turned on and tuned in by the power of emotion. They described themselves as being emotionally connected in values, character, and behavior. Given their professed value for human dignity, equality and diversity, service to others, and making a difference in the world, they were characteristically passionate about serving others toward the achievement of compelling purpose. To that end, they engaged in multiple centering behaviors to emotionally focus and sustain organizational commitment to purpose. It was through such self-described character and behavior, moreover, that they revealed a leadership performance sense of when and how to ease, excite, or evaluate emotional states of mind in themselves and in others.

The leaders' collective reflections suggested a good performance sense of minimizing emotional stress arising from concern for physical or social welfare. Consequently, they cast themselves as characteristically respectful, empathetic, and trustworthy. They also described how they worked to acclimate and match members within their organizations. The leaders further perceived that human capacity is aroused and focused by emotional assessment of what merits effort and that such emotional arousal must be managed to motivational advantage by rational reflection. Thus, they observed how they informed, dialogued, modeled, empowered, and challenged to establish and sustain not only emotional connections to people but also emotional connections between people and purpose.

A Reflective Connection

The interviewed leaders were thinkers who provoked thinking in others. They perceived themselves to be contemplative in character and attentive to the thinking of others in behavior. Again, such self-perception was consistent with the leaders' espoused values for human dignity, equality and diversity, service to others, and making a difference in the world. Such values could hardly be actualized if one did not appreciate and nurture the defining quality of humankind, that is, the capacity for reflective reasoning.

MANIPULATED TO ADVANTAGE

The fundamental genius underlying human capacity is an exceptional ability for constructing and reflectively manipulating useful information patterns.

The human brain is a biological platform of extraordinary capacity for constructing meaning and memory from diverse information sources. We construct knowledge of the world from sensory input stimulated by environmental experience, and direct, rich experience influences the quality of such construction. Social interaction is a primary source for rich environmental experiences, but emotion also plays an important role in the construction of what we understand and remember. We are aroused by knowledge constructions that are emotionally judged worthy of the time and effort. The construction of meaning and memory is further facilitated by emotional contexts that reference the organization of important information patterns. What is constructed and remembered is continually refined and reconstructed through ongoing examination of relationships to new information. We are advisedly attentive to such knowledge refinement, moreover, as comfort with existing information patterns can engender disregard for the value of new information. To that end, we reflectively manipulate what we have constructed in our mind.

Reflection is the distinguishing dimension of human capacity by which we consciously manipulate information and rehearse options prior to action. It is the means by which we move beyond the construction of what is to the reconstruction of what has been and the projection of what might be. To do this, the reflective process incorporates an executive function that purposefully accesses and coordinates the vast resources of our brain in the exercise of complex reasoning. Reflection also performs a governing role as it constrains, redirects, or otherwise remedies actions initiated in other brain areas, particularly actions initiated in the emotional centers of our brain. Ultimately, this capacity for reflective reasoning underlies the scientific, philosophical, and artistic inquiry that empowers human versatility and, thereby, our potential.

SUBJECT TO LEADERSHIP INFLUENCE

Reflection is our species' specialty. It is what allows us to learn from the past and plan for the future. As such, it is the most promising dimension within our overall capacity for learning and achieving. The ability to imagine, improvise, plan ahead, and reflect on possible results is key to our versatility and survival. Because we are able to continually entertain new ideas and processes with flexibility and foresight, we enjoy enormous advantage in weathering challenges, both as individuals and as communities.

The importance of cultivating reflective thinking in the self and others should be of fairly obvious leadership concern. Given that reflection is a determining factor in how far and well we travel neural pathways toward life success, we might appreciate that such capacity is realized only to the degree that there is a productive disposition driving it.

Encouragingly, as you are aware from reading the preceding chapters, the 36 interviewed leaders were quite aware of their reflective capacity and also well disposed toward both exercising and promoting such capacity through their leadership performance. Again, their reflections in this area were very compatible with their core values for human dignity, equality and diversity, service to others, and making a difference in the world. In both character and behavior, they described a propensity for engaging the minds of others in productive reflection. Toward that end, they were humbly respectful, empathetic, and straightforward in promoting ongoing dialogue that both informed and challenged thinking within their organizations. They were also inclined to model reflective contemplation and to empower others to engage in such reflection both individually and in teams.

Through their portrayal of their force of character across specific fields of behavior, the leaders presented a picture of a strong performance connection to the reflective capacity of self and others. Their stories described many instances in which they aspired to facilitate the construction and refinement of knowledge. They were particularly attentive to involving associates in problem solving, decision making, conflict resolving, and other exercises of analytic and creative thinking.

Most important, the leaders' collective reflections suggested a strong appreciation for cultivating productive habits of thinking that would maximize people's capacity for achievement over time. They also voiced appreciation for the fact that such habits of mind would only evolve to the degree that they were frequently exercised.

Lessons Learned

The self-described performance of these 36 interviewed leaders portrays them as a social, emotional, and reflective group. Furthermore, what they embodied in themselves is what they nurtured in others. They conducted their leadership business in a manner that consistently advanced social, emotional, and reflective connections to those they aspired to influence toward the achievement of goals.

> "The world we live in from day to day is, for the most part, composed of other people, and what they think and feel has great consequence to us."
>
> —Ornstein (1997, p. 121)

This matter of capacity connections is of particular interest as it portrays the human face of leadership. It speaks to a performance orientation that appreciates the importance of being, feeling, and thinking with the people one is attempting to influence toward the achievement of goals. The interviewed leaders' orientation to social, emotional, and reflective relationships also reflects theories that attribute effective leadership influence to qualities of traits, knowledge, and contingent behavior (Antonakis, et al., 2004). Such orientation is particularly consistent with the themes described in the research on transformational leadership (Sashkin, 2004). In attending to the social, emotional, and reflective nature of relationships, the 36 leaders portray leadership performance that "looks for potential motives in followers, seeks to meet higher needs and engages the full person" (Burns, 1978, p. 4). They cast themselves as transformational leaders oriented to "influence based on persuasion rather than coercion, driven by higher concern for the persons involved than mere goal attainments" (Rost, 1993, p. 124). This is all the more noteworthy given that transformational, rather than transactional leadership (i.e., oriented toward bartering of power and resources) has been found as the preferred leadership style across many countries and cultures (Bass, 1997), as well as the more effective style overall. (Center for Leadership Studies, 2000; Lowe et al., 1996).

What have we learned about capacity-connected leadership performance from this group of leaders? That might reasonably be reduced to five items that reference insights across Chapters 4 through 6.

1. Leadership performance necessarily emerges from how one is formed as a leader. This does not infer that leadership performance is not malleable, only that there are influential origins behind who we are and how we act as leaders.

2. Leadership performance emanates from force of character and fields of behavior aligned to core values.

3. Leadership benefits from performance that is humble, passionate, and contemplative in character.

4. Leadership benefits from performance behaviors that build community, center purpose and process, and promote thinking.

5. Congruency between leadership values, character, and behavior forges leadership connections to the social, emotional, and reflective dimensions of human capacity for growth and achievement.

As we move on in this leadership story, then, we have additional information from 36 leaders' perceptions about leadership as a process of influencing others toward the achievement of a goal. Specifically, leadership performance has been examined as the "how" piece of the equation. The apparent lesson of note is that coherent leadership follows an observable path from formation to performance. How leaders are formed exerts strong influence on how leadership is performed through force of character and fields of behavior. What the leaders valued was in natural and logical agreement with who they were and what they did—and who they were and what they did forged a social, emotional, and reflective leadership influence on others (see Figure 7.1).

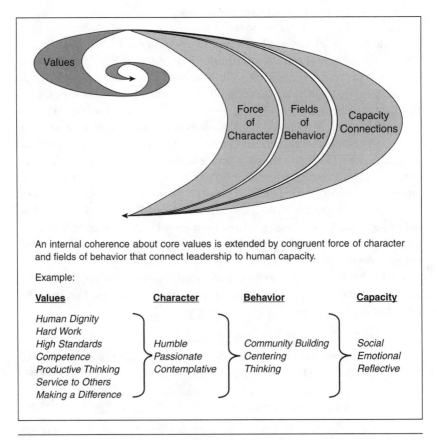

An internal coherence about core values is extended by congruent force of character and fields of behavior that connect leadership to human capacity.

Example:

Values	Character	Behavior	Capacity
Human Dignity Hard Work High Standards Competence Productive Thinking Service to Others Making a Difference	Humble Passionate Contemplative	Community Building Centering Thinking	Social Emotional Reflective

Figure 7.1   Leadership Coherence Promotes Performance Connections to Capacity

Further Conversation

As you rejoin this leadership conversation at this juncture, the conversation invites reflection about leadership performance connections to social, emotional, and reflective dimensions of human capacity for growth and achievement. This is an opportunity to assess how you nurture such connections in the process of influencing others toward the achievement of goals. Your participation in the conversation will be facilitated by the following Further Conversation exercise (again, to be conducted either individually or in the company of colleagues, as you prefer).

EXERCISE 7.1 Further Conversation: Capacity Connections

A. Why might leadership connections to the social nature of human capacity be important?

B. How does your leadership character and behavior promote productive social relationships in your organization?

C. Why might leadership connections to the emotional nature of human capacity be important?

D. How does your leadership character and behavior promote productive emotional states in your organization?

E. Why might leadership connections to the reflective nature of human capacity be important?

F. How does your leadership character and behavior promote productive reflection and reasoning in your organization?

Part III

Leadership Sustained

Very little in our lives is more important and more pervasive than our relationships with those we care about and with whom we work. And very little is more inscrutable and problematic.

—Barth (2003, p. xi)

Two primary components of a coherent leadership model are now on the table. Notably, the stories shared by 36 leaders portray a dynamic and congruent relationship between leadership formation and performance. We now move on to frame a third component of coherent leadership, that of leadership sustainability. Within this conversation, the leaders describe dispositions that compound leadership influence and legacy, as well as strategies that sustain the leader behind the leadership.

8

Sustaining Dispositions

In humans the long process of evolution has produced a species of problem solvers, happiest when engaged in tasks that require not only physical effort, but also the engagement of mind and heart. We are not only problem solvers but also problem seekers.

—Gardner (1990, p. 195)

The Nature of Dispositions

The third question in the interview protocol prompted reflection about leadership sustainability. In response, the eclectic group of 36 exemplary leaders described defining leadership dispositions—habitual inclinations of character and behavior that both sustained and compounded their leadership influence.

As previously defined in Chapter 4, character is the peculiar quality, or sum of qualities, by which a person is distinguished from others. It is the unique stamp imprinted by the interaction of nature, education, or habit that describes that which a person really is. It is also a term used to describe a person's attributes, traits, or abilities, particularly those associated with moral or ethical strength and principles that motivate and direct one's life. Such definition, moreover, embraces a general understanding of the nature of dispositions as tendencies, inclinations, or habits of thinking and acting.

With the above definitions in mind, our conversation now turns to how leadership is sustained. The interviewed leaders describe how they aspired to an enduring influence on the achievement of goals. It is a conversation that also sheds light on how leaders continue to learn, grow, and maintain their physical and mental well-being while enduring difficult challenges and setbacks. It is through such insights that a distinction emerges between influential character traits and sustaining leadership dispositions. Specifically, it would appear that force of character (as examined in Chapter 5) is a defining element of leadership performance. Beyond character traits that express core values in everyday performance, however, there are dispositions that form the sustaining backbone of leadership influence over time. As such, dispositions represent refined leadership qualities of character and enable a prevailing and lasting leadership effect.

AS WE ARE DISPOSED, SO IT GOES

Dispositions are habitual patterns of thinking and acting that are rooted in our genetic infrastructure. At the same time, such habitual patterns are highly malleable by life experience. Variously referred to as habits, tendencies, inclinations, attitudes, personality, character, or temperament, dispositions are observable in every arena of human activity. They serve as behavior templates that affect hygiene, exercise, diet, interpersonal relations, work, and virtually any other activity that allows for an option as to how to act. Simply put, dispositions shape our lives. "They are proclivities that lead us in one direction rather than another within the freedom of action that we have" (Perkins, 1995, p. 275).

> "Divide the world into energy givers and energy consumers. It is the energy consumers who will find a cloud for every silver lining."
>
> —Tim Brighouse

Indeed, it is difficult to imagine human existence without the element of habitual behavior. Life would be considerably more difficult to manage on a moment-to-moment basis if we had to continually pause to reflect about each and every behavior option. The establishment of habitual behavior patterns relieves our brain of the mundane preoccupation of how to act in every instance. The trick, of course, is to establish productive dispositions that generally guide advantageous survival behavior over the wide range of human activity. For example, advantage might be realized from being disposed to be persistent, creative, open-minded, organized, or analytical as opposed to being weak-willed, unimaginative, closed-minded, disorganized, and unquestioning.

The bottom line is that there is no choice in the matter of fundamental human dispositions. It is natural for us to habitually interact socially with others as a means to learn and achieve, to emotionally arouse our mind and body to advantageous actions, to construct and store useful information patterns from the richness of environmental experience, and to consciously reflect about objectives, obstacles, and options. It is our nature to be so disposed. It is as natural as breathing.

There is considerable latitude, nevertheless, in how well we nurture and exercise that which is natural. This is so because—as influenced by nature or nurture or a combination thereof—we judge some habitual patterns of thinking and acting to be of survival value. This does not mean that a particular pattern is indeed a good one in a particular time and place; it just means that we, at some level, believe that it is (i.e., to be positive, open-minded, adventurous, trusting, proactive). Furthermore, as Dewey (1933, p. 89) advised, "Mental habits, whether good or bad, are certain to be formed." The question to be addressed, then, is whether and how we form quality habits. How well will we attend to what condition our disposition is in?

THE BACKBONE OF LEADERSHIP

Returning to an earlier (i.e., Chapter 4) analogy of a chiropractor attending to issues of body alignment, it is useful to weigh the merits of systemic attention to such alignment over time. It is instructive in visualizing the alignment of particular parts of a system, your back or neck, for example. Such attention to a misaligned portion of the body is effective and appreciated in the short run. It is attention to total body system alignment over time, however, that trains muscle memory and habituates the way we maintain agility and freedom from pain.

This analogy serves our understanding of a leader's interest in ministering to productive dispositions in self and others. Productive thinking habits, in particular, are determining influences on how effectively we access our potential. Human capacity to learn and achieve is realized to the degree that there is a productive disposition driving it. Indeed, it is dispositions that either maximize or minimize the exercise of intelligent and productive behavior in individuals and organizations. For that reason, a leader would be understandably attentive to productive dispositions as the means to best nurture the alignment of human capacity and meaningful purpose. Indeed, this arguably represents the backbone of leadership, that is, what leaders will attend to if they aspire to establish and sustain a systemic exercise of organizational intelligence behavior over time.

> "What is the satisfaction of leadership? For me it is always seeing others, for whom one has an organizational responsibility, flourish and succeed at the things they are here to pursue and do. That's really how I get my thrill out of this role, in seeing others do very, very well, and to create the environment where they can."
>
> —John Hood

Such leadership attention to the cultivation of productive dispositions is reinforced across a wide range of scholarship about qualities of effective thinking and behavior. Notably, scholars in this arena have posited the distinction between human capacity and thinking dispositions that take full advantage of said capacity. Examples include Covey's (1989) conclusion that highly effective people are proactive, look to the end, put first things first, seek first to understand, then be understood, seek win-win solutions, synergize, and pursue physical, social-emotional, mental, and spiritual self-renewal. Similarly, Costa and

Kallick (2000) described 16 habits of mind displayed by good thinkers in response to problems, dilemmas, and enigmas (i.e., persisting, managing impulsivity, listening with understanding and empathy, thinking flexibly, thinking about thinking [metacognition], striving for accuracy, questioning and posing problems, applying past knowledge to new problems, thinking and communicating with clarity and precision, gathering data with all senses, creating and innovating, responding with wonderment and awe, taking responsible risks, finding humor, thinking interdependently, and remaining open to continuous learning). Perkins (1995) and Marzano and Pickering (1997) are other describers of effective thinking qualities. Senge (1990) adds description of the qualities of systems thinking, personal mastery, mental models, shared vision, and team learning in learning organizations.

With perspective of their import, then, quality dispositions of mind and behavior will be attended to first and foremost by leaders who are serious about influencing individual and organizational capacity toward the achievement of goals. Indeed, the importance of dispositions conjures up the classic axiom about teaching a man how to fish so that he might feed himself for a lifetime versus giving a man a fish to feed him for a day. If dispositions of mind and behavior are mandatory, yet malleable, influences on how well we exercise our capacities, a leader is well advised to focus on the cultivation of productive habits. It is the systemic nurture of productive dispositions throughout the culture of an organization that ultimately compounds and sustains leadership influence.

With this background about the nature of dispositions in mind, the following sections note how the 36 leaders revealed themselves to be strongly disposed toward the nurture of sustaining dispositions in the self and others.

Seven Defining Dispositions

The reflections of 36 leaders about leadership sustainability generated rich conversation about how they were fundamentally disposed to engage life's challenges and opportunities. From that conversation, seven prominent dispositions emerged that were deemed important to an enduring and profound leadership influence. Specifically, the collective insight of the leaders advocated for the dispositions of being centered, analytic, creative, positive, persistent, curious, and invested.

These were dispositions of distinction—important qualities to be exercised, developed, and reinforced within both the leader and the culture. They were dispositions that leaders embodied, modeled, and otherwise promoted as the means to both sustain and compound leadership influence on others toward the achievement of compelling goals. Most important, they were dispositions that taught others "how to fish." Cultivated throughout an organizational culture, these dispositions encouraged sustainability of progress through an organizational intelligence that appropriately diminished dependence on the capacities of the leader alone. Richard Teerlink, for example, credited the sustainability of Harley-Davidson to such a cultural shift: "My biggest contribution at Harley was culture. We had to change the way we worked together. It is the responsibility of leaders to insure the long-term viability of the enterprise." Thus, in this discernment of important dispositions, the 36 leaders were also acknowledging a leadership responsibility for nurturing capacity in individuals and groups throughout the organization.

CENTERED

Not surprisingly, the 36 interviewed leaders were strongly disposed to focus on what was most central to their purpose.

Roger Harmon often employed elements of an ancient folk ritual, the "Baci" or "Soul Calling" ceremony of Laos and Northeast Thailand. The traditional ceremony combines Buddhist, Hindu, and Animist elements and is led by a chanter who calls "home" the 32 "minor" souls of a celebrant. The celebrant is blessed before undergoing an important life event or transition or on returning home to family and friends after being away. Once the chanter has called back the souls, their return

> "I believe in the power of truth. I'm not afraid to lose."
>
> — *Richard Bissen*

is symbolized by well-wishers who tie cotton strings around the wrists of the celebrant and give him or her their wishes of friendship and tidings of happiness, health, and strength. Participants then tie strings on each other and again share their wishes for health and happiness. This reaffirms the bonds of the assembled family and community group.

On some occasions, a traditional chanter performs the entire ceremony. More often, however, much of the ritual is pared away, and the centering, connecting "essence" of the ceremony is sought through a brief description of the ceremony and its purposes. Participants are still invited to tie cotton string and express positive wishes and connections for and between individuals of the group. Regardless of whether the ceremony is traditional and "full-blown" or greatly modified, Roger felt that participants always experience an event of significance.

Roger referenced the Baci tradition and otherwise worked to stay centered and focused on what he perceived to be the most important part of his role of supporting Peace Corps volunteers in the field. His concern was that a given administration in Washington, D.C., might waver from the central mission of the Peace Corps.

> Volunteers have come up to me and said that I really helped them link into why they came. As long as there are Peace Corps directors who will keep the

focus front and center, I'm not worried about the Peace Corps becoming a political arm. People need leaders who will keep helping them [connect] to why they came and what the fundamental goals are all about. It is very easy to get lost out there in the day to day.

Conversations about core purpose were deemed essential by other leaders to enhance the drive to achieve within employees. As Richard Teerlink noted, one can't take purpose for granted.

> I believe it is so important for workers to know their purpose. I always use the example of accounts payable. What's their purpose? They would say to pay the bills. I would say why don't we look at it differently. Your job is to insure that our processes don't jeopardize our relationship with a good supplier. [With such perspective,] they will do a much better job on a day in and day out basis. If people have a chance to talk about it, they will find their purpose much deeper than they initially thought.

It was abundantly clear that all of the interviewed leaders carried their personal sense of purpose to the heart of their decision making. Their relentless drive to fulfill their mission was precipitated by a deep, central purpose. Ian Fox, for example, was quite aware of the influence that emanated from his driving intent.

> I think I'm quite a focused leader. I've always, for years and years, had this mental picture of a perfect school. I'm not quite sure that I can put into words what that perfect school is, but I've always had this vision of a perfect school where, if people just enjoyed it. . . . It's such a neat place to be, kids are happy, teachers are happy, learning outcomes are there. The whole thing works really well. I think I am quite focused in terms of trying to create something that is closer to the vision. It's very elusive to get there, but that's what visions are, that's the exciting challenge. If we have a difficult decision to make, we go back to our core belief. It's paramount that the focus is on students first. So, how does this benefit students? One of our other core beliefs is that we value teachers as our best resource, so it can't be bad for teachers. But if we have to make a choice as to a decision we're making, then we go back to that first principle, "Is this the best option for the students?" There's a quote, something along the lines of "It's not what the leader does, but what the leader stands for." I think it's true.

Sometimes a leader's commitment to remaining centered created conflict with others, but as Nola Hambleton observed, drifting from the center was not an option.

> I am a visionary and I have arguments with people who talk about shared visions. I think that is great, you've got to have a shared vision, but you can

equally have a vision for yourself and know where you are going. Here, at this school, I've got a vision of raising the standards and making this a place for children to come to where they can not only enjoy their environment but know that they are going to learn as well. Along the way, I appoint people who are going to share my vision. I say this to young principals all of the time. . . . It's getting people on board that share your view, talking and discussing and persuading them. I have to have people with me. I talk about it and I discuss a lot. But that doesn't mean I do everything as a team. There are times when I have a very fixed view that I know is absolutely right and I would not hesitate to go through with that.

Finding and connecting with others who shared their central purpose was a common theme throughout most of the leaders' conversations. Jeanne Dukes illustrated this theme with comments that echoed those of Nola Hambleton.

I think the critical issue in leadership is the ability to know what your vision and mission are and then fit your staffing to meet that vision. That means the kind of people that will get you there, and the talents that will get you there, and the intelligence that will get you there. You have to know what works for you and your vision and then you go and find it. You can't be willy-nilly, and you can't let other people run your program. Others will think they know, and they don't. Sometimes people in the larger organization get frustrated with me, but as long as I'm running this program, it's going to look like this. You have to believe in yourself and your bedrock values. You can't equivocate and try to please everybody.

Underlying the leaders' disposition to be strongly centered (as should come as no surprise at this point in our conversation) was their connection to their core values—values that they naturally applied to their leadership context. Central to Denese Henare's work, for example, was her value for Maori heritage.

My work is focused on understanding values and meaning within certain contexts. I work to make institutions more sensitive to Maori beliefs and traditions. The Waitanga treaty has survived due to its moral significance and increasingly more political significance. The value and culture of Maori must be honored. Now is a chapter in a long journey. In this day of globalization, how does one retain a sense of self and one's values?

The disposition of the 36 leaders was to be strongly centered on vision and mission aligned to core values. Such disposition helped both leaders and associates sustain resolve and reinforce confidence in the directions set for the leaders' organizations. As Beth Stevenson said, "I look inside to my core values. What do I need to do to live with myself? You have to discover the center within."

ANALYTIC

Leadership is a process of influencing others toward the achievement of goals. Generally, the "achievement of goals" portion of that definition translates into problems to be resolved and tasks to be completed. It is only helpful, therefore, if a leader is disposed to analytic thinking—inclined to examine the pieces, explore options, seek solutions, and to otherwise generally "figure it out." As might be expected, the interviewed leaders were so disposed. Ian Fox, for example, learned from a mentor that no one is going to solve problems for you.

> "I figure things out pretty quickly. I thrive on problem-solving situations."
>
> *— Richard Bissen*

> So the lesson wasn't how he solved the problem, but that you have to solve the problem yourself. That was a good lesson. He gave me a lot of freedom and latitude that enabled me to develop areas of interest and strength. If I saw something in the school that I felt could be changed or have an impact, then he would accept the idea, allow me to run with the idea and do something with it. I've developed some strategies when a problem occurs. I get very focused. If I have a major problem, I probably get more withdrawn than normal, pull back a bit, until my mind is clear and I know what I've got to do to deal with the problem and the sequence of events. I try to communicate with people so that [they] know what's happening.

The interviewed leaders understood that not only would others generally not solve problems for them, but also they would not be the only source of problem solving for others. Richard Teerlink learned this lesson as a young supervisor.

> I look back on one of my early jobs as supervisor when I thought that I was there to be their problem solver. I had no training as a supervisor but had been trained as an accountant, a problem solver. So I thought my job was to check in with everybody and find out if I could help. I had an individual look up one time and say, "Rich, don't you have enough to do?" "Well what do you mean?" I said. "You're hovering over me. Understand one thing. We had a good department before you came. We are going to have an excellent department while you are here, and we're going to have an excellent department after you leave." What that said to me was that my job was not to be a problem solver for others, but to make sure they had the resources to solve their own problems.

For many leaders, the focus was not the problem per se, but rather a solution that engaged others in moving the organization toward its goals. Energy was to be turned to positive resolve. Rod Chamberlain commented on his experience with this approach.

There is often a barrier. But to get past that barrier, there is usually one little thing. That one thing may look huge, initially, but it's not that huge. So my job is to help people with that one little thing. The fun is sitting there and watching that happen. The joy of Kamehameha School is watching the process. I am dealing with a $6 billion company. We have been talking through the process of continuous improvement. So it's a joy to see how many things I can influence and in the end, they will say, "We worked this out pretty well."

Finding solutions that were systemic and oriented to long-term resolution was also important. Gabor Halmai observed the need to analyze the bigger picture.

At our human rights center, people came in with legal problems, human rights problems, and we gave advice to them. I realized that there is not much sense doing the work that way because 90% of the cases were hopeless. I decided to change the whole system, to reverse the procedure. I have an ambition to solve problems, and this is the reason why I have accepted all these obligations that really are too much. I think the most important thing, at all three places I work, is to find out the mission of the organization and the most important tools to fulfill this mission. I came here, for instance, to change the functioning of the organization, to concentrate on some really important things to help this foundation work. Ultimately, I had to decide to make more policy than program.

In the process of creating a culture shift at Harley-Davidson, Rich Teerlink determined that assisting others with critical-thinking skills was essential. The results, as he noted, changed the tone within the organization.

We identified ahead of time how we would work together. When you teach union leaders conflict resolution and problem solving, you change the tenor of the conversation. At Harley, we offer conflict resolution and problem-solving courses for people to take. We don't mandate it, because people need to take responsibly for their own learning.

Thus, the interviewed leaders were disposed to continually analyze challenges and the means to their resolution. They were not only disposed to embrace such a role for themselves, but also to encourage like disposition in others as a means to sustain progress toward organizational goals.

CREATIVE

The 36 leaders described an important relationship between the disposition of being analytic and the complimentary disposition of being creative. Analyzing and seeking resolution or advantage from problems or opportunities most often benefited from the leaders' inclination to be innovative in their thinking.

> "You can't change the wind, but you can adjust your sails. If you can't find a path, then you make one."
>
> —CJ Nickerson

Working for a large bureaucracy early in his career helped CJ Nickerson develop a disposition for creative problem solving. As a School Health Supervisor for a State Department of Education, CJ was frustrated by the internal structures and policies that impeded his work. He came to the realization that the only way to sustain and build health education programs was if health educators took control of their own destiny. This required money. He and two other colleagues investigated great opportunities and determined that they did not give money to state agencies.

> We were walking back to my office and I said, "You know, I don't see anybody that wants to give money to the state, but they do give money to nonprofits and private foundations. I'm wondering why we don't just create our own foundation." They both gave me that deer-in-the-headlights stare, and I went home and slept on it. The more I thought about it, the more excited I became.

Such was the genesis of what eventually became a $30 million health education foundation.

The interviewed leaders also often observed the importance of thinking and acting in revolutionary ways. In Mechai Viraviadya's view, his homeland government needed to be transformed dramatically.

> Let the women run Thailand for a while, because the men have ruined it long enough. I have 4 more years to do it, to try to get through a constitutional amendment where half of the elected officials would be women. In each electorate, you would vote for two: one man and one woman. Thailand would be a much better place, believe me. The women keep the villages together [and] have much better ideas in terms of what to do to make lives better for people, whereas the men are materialistic. Let the pendulum swing the other way for a while.

Mechai also likened challenges to water flowing in a stream that encounters a dam. "It can go around it, over it, or wait to evaporate and come down as rain on the other side." He and the other leaders expressed a strong belief that there was always a way to achieve a worthy goal if given time and creativity.

Donald Gwira's creative disposition was evidenced in his job interview.

> I was asked to come up with a strategy for raising the profile of Sight Savers in the region and abroad. I developed "Sight is precious and we often take it for granted. Close your eyes for a minute and enter the world of the blind. Try moving around. This is what 45 million blind people experience every day."

Donald's idea was so effective that it is now part of the advocacy campaign for Sight Savers International. Donald prized such creativity and purposefully cultivated it.

I have a very imaginative mind. Sometimes I sit for a few minutes and just allow my mind to wander, and all of a sudden I'll get this message. If you ask me now what my next creation would be, I probably would not be able to tell you. It has to occur. But I hope when the next deadline comes, I am ready to deliver.

The disposition to be innovative and assume the accompanying risks often took root in the leaders' early experience. Nola Hambleton talked about developing a tendency to think otherwise.

Earlier in my career, I did some reading, and I read about a school in England where they threw out all of the furniture in the classrooms and the children were sitting on cushions. I thought it would be wonderful to try. So I went to my principal and told him. He was a very wise man. He looked at me for a while and said, "Draw up a proposal." So I did and came back to him and he said, "Well, I'm going to let you try this on the condition that if it doesn't work, you must come and tell me immediately. You must not say, 'I'm going to make it work.'" It didn't work. So that was something I learned. You've got to be prepared to say if it worked or not. He allowed me to be innovative.

Innovation was also exhibited in the leaders' tendency to enjoy the start-up of new ventures. Gabor Halmai described such satisfaction.

I went to the Central European University to be Director of the newly established human rights program there. It was very interesting to create something from nothing. There was no human rights education at the CEU before, so I established this program and led it. That led to the Dutch Foreign Ministry establishing a human rights information documentation center to help lawyers dealing with human rights cases. We organized conferences; training for judges, prosecutors, and attorneys; and began a human rights quarterly, which was a journal on various human rights issues.

A preference for work that allowed for innovation was common to the leaders. Mechai Viraviadya, again, described the importance of innovation to the moneymaking ventures and corporate alliances that funded his NGO's efforts to improve public health.

When I look back, I didn't see it at the time. I think I like areas that are more creative. I think I preferred to work in an area where there would be room for some adaptations, adjustments, and changes. PDA [Population Development Association] is still doing public work. I call it the privatization of policy reduction, getting the business sector involved, taking the right approach to it. In most of the world, you cannot expect to get money given to you forever. You must have other ingenuities, be financially independent. Just like a new baby coming along, everything else has a limited period in terms of mother's milk.

As did the other leaders, Mechai saw himself as innovative and thought this was a key ingredient to leadership success. Alex Banful described taking such perspective to work. "If you ask most people, they would tell you that this is my small laboratory and I test all kinds of methodologies here. I consider this office to be a school." Beth Stevenson was even more aggressive about this point.

> I am very creative and operate from an entrepreneurial viewpoint. I don't like maintenance and recognize that I'm not good at it. You can never be truly in maintenance because your goal is always in the future.

POSITIVE

Coherence began to emerge within the self-described dispositions of the 36 leaders. Centered on their vision and mission, they were naturally and logically disposed to be analytic and creative in acting on that vision and mission. Moreover, the leaders were not disposed to view problems as restraints or obstacles but rather to see them as opportunities for improvement and progress. The Chinese symbol for crisis,

> "I believe that people are trying to do good."
>
> — Beth Stevenson

which can be either interpreted as challenge or opportunity, speaks to such orientation to problems. The leaders did not see a cup half full; they saw a cup that was overflowing with opportunity. They were overwhelmingly positive in their dispositions. Perhaps the most dramatic example of such a positive leadership outlook came from Kuami Pianim, who spent 10 of his most productive adult years in jail as a political prisoner. Rather than regretting what had happened to him, he was able to look back on this incredible hardship as a gift to his soul that both clarified and strengthened his current resolve to rebuild Ghana.

Working with cast-out students in a large county school district, Jeanne Dukes encountered the underbelly of society on a daily basis: desperate children afflicted by broken homes, drugs abuse, crime, and illicit sex. Her positive disposition formed the bedrock of her ability to keep doing her work well.

> There has to be an element of belief in the goodness of the world, that even though bad things happen, there is a reason to create another generation. It took me 10 years to recover from the upheaval [I experienced] as a teenager and to realize that there were good things as well.

Tim Brighouse developed a personal "energy-giving" model to drive his leadership.

> It starts with what's good and trying to spread it. It's not fixing problems, it's spreading goodness. I divide the world into energy givers and energy

consumers. It is the energy consumers who will find a cloud for every silver lining. I have an optimistic view and believe that you can build on the good.

From a pragmatic perspective, Richard Teerlink demonstrated his positive outlook while questioning what is routine practice in most organizations: performance evaluation.

> I believe that most negative performance evaluations happen when leadership has failed. Anytime an employee has to be terminated, most of the blame rests with leadership rather than the employee. I honestly believe that no one comes to work wanting to do a bad job. If they do a bad job, it's probably because something was missing. At Harley, we have a process called PEP, not performance evaluation process, because nobody wants to be evaluated. I said, "Why don't we call it performance effectiveness process?" Let's focus our conversation on how they can be effective and ask them.

Bob Knight summed up his positive disposition as a philosophy of leadership and a way of life.

> I believe that it is up to you. My philosophy is, "Life is good," and that attitude creates success. I believe leadership is about outlook and demeanor. If you are positive, you will earn respect and enjoy the challenge as well as the results.

PERSISTENT

The 36 leaders had both the mental toughness and the fortitude to persist when the chips were down and solutions elusive. All had faced hardships early on in life that honed their values and vocational callings. Such hardships also prepared them to handle difficult challenges further along their leadership path. Over time, they developed the inner strength to persist with confidence toward compelling goals.

Kuami Pianim was sentenced to 18 years as a political prisoner in Ghana. During the 10 years he ended up serving, he both persisted and grew in his convictions.

> "I think it came from my family, that if you start something, you should finish it."
>
> —Margo Dévai

> I belong to the Asanti tribe. We are very independent and never work for the government. As a result of a military coup, they took me to a tribunal and sent me to jail. When there was a return to civil rule, I was freed. But while in prison, I realized that about 50% of the people who were there were there because they were poor, not because they were guilty.

Compelled by his values and experience, Kuami started a poultry farm that created work for the prisoners, taught them work skills they could use on their release, and made money for the government. That initiative grew into a tree farm and an educational program. As a result, when Kuami was released, he was motivated to continue what he had started. "I became quite politicized and committed to continuing to work for the economic development of Ghana, and still do to this day."

Prior to becoming the principal at his present school, Ian Fox had moved up his career ladder fairly quickly. He had, however, chosen to stay in his current position for a considerable length of time.

> I've been here 16 years, and in the midst of this whole process, it worries me that I won't recognize when it's time to go. That's a worry, and maybe it drives me also. I'm still here, and I think the exciting part is I have been here a significant length of time. I've tried to develop something, and the challenge for me is how far can you go with a school, how far can you take it? I think mostly we've built a successful school, and our results would show that. There have been some exciting things happening, and I think there are still. I can still see that this year is going to be better than last year. As long as I can keep seeing that, I feel okay.

Ian also shared that he had had job offers that attempted to lure him away but that his commitment to the school's vision had kept him in place for the long haul.

Maintaining a perspective of the big picture helped Patrick Sayne persist in his leadership efforts.

> You figure out that the sun is going to rise in the East, no matter what happens. You don't want to give up, but you want to adopt an attitude that there is always another day. A key issue is persistence. Most leaders weren't unqualified successes their whole life. They had to go through some adversity, and maybe this was necessary. Churchill wasn't anointed. You have to learn to lose too.

Motivated by their passion for their vision and mission, the leaders resisted complacency. One of Mechai Viraviadya's greatest challenges required such vigilance. As a result of his efforts, Thailand was one of the first two countries in the world to reduce the incidence of AIDS in the early stages of the global crisis. When asked if he was able to sustain such effects, Mechai was assertive.

> In the last 10 years, new cases have declined by about 77%. In the last couple of years, [it has been] a bit slow, so I pushed it again from the outside. The Prime Minister understands that this is a major issue that we really have to work hard with. People think that AIDS has gone away. We've got to keep it alive, like Coca Cola. When you take a look at a situation, when you say you must not give up, it forces you to think more dynamically and widely. When you know you cannot accept defeat for a cause, then you look at every avenue.

The leaders' disposition to be persistent in pursuit of meaningful goals was also apparent in their work ethic. The old adage "Hard work pays off" was a shared perspective that sustained them through long days and difficult tasks. For most, the orientation to working hard ran deep. Ian Fox was aware of the work ethic that fueled his approach to the principalship and the expectations he held for his staff.

> I think if I try to be analytical about myself and my background, it's probably a Presbyterian work ethic and upbringing that comes from my grandfather's side, who was a very stern Scottish Presbyterian. I don't know that it was a conscious thing, but I was always in awe of my grandfather.

Alex Banful was a bit more blunt in commenting, "My work is a member of my family, just after my wife and kids." Rod Chamberlain was somewhat more philosophical in describing his nonstop commitment to his work.

> There are blue-collar, white-collar, and gold-collar people. Gold-collar people love their work so much that you are engaged in it all the time. You are thinking about it all the time. And it's wonderful . . . you get paid to do it.

The disposition to persist and work hard was, nevertheless, often challenged by the magnitude of the work to be done. Not one, not two, but three demanding leadership positions commanded Gabor Halmai's full-time attention. With a new wife who also wanted his attention, he was torn between his commitment to values of social justice and trying to find a healthy balance for himself as well.

> When I accepted this job in September [as Director of Soros in Hungary], I accepted with the condition that I would like to keep my other two jobs. So I have three jobs now. Sometimes I have the feeling that it is too much. It's really three different challenging things. The most disturbing thing that I realized after coming back to Hungary, after being away at Princeton, is that the whole atmosphere has been changed, and a strong right-wing movement is present. There is open anti-Semitism in Hungary. If the foundation can do anything about this bad tendency, then this is the time and the last minute [to do it]. So even though I know that this is too much, I have accepted it.

The disposition to persist and work hard influenced the leaders' modeling behaviors. Mechai shared his sentiments on this issue.

> I'm a taskmaster, known to set goals. There's a very keen line between what is right and what is wrong. It is not a gray area. So we must deliver. We promise quality in terms of integrity, which is also very important. We don't want anything that is shady in what we do. Don't just give an order; follow up, monitor, and walk around. Let your shoes wear out before your pants.

Long hours and persistent effort were important to both Bob Knight and Frank Lukasavitz not only as a way to accomplish the work, but also as a means to model for others. Bob felt strongly about providing a good example.

I try to lead by example. I am one of the first to get here and the last to leave. I do it to get things done, but I am a firm believer that this builds respect. Other leaders may come in around nine and leave at three, but that doesn't build respect.

Beyond living and modeling a life of hard work, Frank frequently encouraged his students with one of his sincere beliefs about what made the difference between success and failure: "The more you practice, the luckier you get. It's about hard work."

Ulice Payne provided an insightful summary observation about the theme of persistence in sharing his philosophy of leadership. "Leadership is about what you do when it doesn't go as well as when it does. Leadership is about showing up. You're there every day."

CURIOUS

Lifelong learning was more than a cliché for the 36 leaders, as they conveyed an unquenchable thirst for new insights and challenges. They actively sought stimulation through the engagement of new information and ideas. Ian Fox was turned on by the change and challenge associated with his work.

I think I've always enjoyed the excitement of education. Even the bad times are exciting. The adrenaline starts running, and things move. You make a decision and go. You have to communicate the decision, let everyone know, deal with the phone calls, try to make everybody comfortable about the reasons behind why, and ride it through. It's the storm before the calm again. I think if I can see a crisis is developing, I want to deal with it quickly [and] minimize the risk and impact. I want to be honest and open about it, share the information so people know why the decisions are being made, and let everybody know the problem and where we are going.

> "Leadership will stagnate without curiosity."
>
> —Patrick Sayne

Patrick Sayne offered a similar perspective.

I also think leaders are hyperactive, maybe adrenaline junkies. Some of us are turned on by the constant change and varied routine. Someone recently did a study where she followed a group of superintendents around to see what they did. She discovered that their days were characterized by many interactions of short duration. The likelihood that you would do this [be a superintendent] for 24 years if you didn't like it is slim to none.

Helen Clark also expressed value for the constant change and challenge she encountered in her role as Prime Minister. "If I leave, it would be due to boredom, not stress."

Nola Hambleton saw challenges as opportunities for investigation and self-improvement.

> I am constantly looking for new ideas. I'm constantly seeking to improve myself as a leader, but also the results of my leadership. The challenges must be there for me, and I'm motivated by them. I'm lucky that I enjoy challenges. I actually get bored in the holidays after a little while if I don't have something to do. Always in my life, I need to have something else to strive for, no matter if it's in my personal or working life. At the present time, I do a lot of reading and discussing with other colleagues. I'm in a principal quality circle of about six principals and we meet twice a term. We have a topic, and everybody looks for reading on it. It's a way of keeping our brains active and thinking educationally and comparing our ideas with someone else.

Rod Chamberlain noted, however, that the trait of innate curiosity was not universal.

> I have been amazed at how many people aren't willing to be open to possibilities. So much of life is being open to possibilities. I think this came from family. My grandparents were missionaries in Jamaica, and they did international ministry. There was a sense of joy in sharing food from Kenya and stories from Taiwan. It was never scary or anxious. When I was a kid—I was born in California—and my dad said, "We are going on a new adventure. We are going to move to New York state." Change was always framed for me as an adventure, which is such a wonderful word versus another word like nightmare.

Julianne Lowe endorsed such openness to new ideas and experience with advice she gave to herself.

> It doesn't matter how much knowledge you have, you are not infallible and can always learn more. They say on the road that if you think you know everything, it is time to leave. Once you stop listening and researching and think that you're right, then you have lost the plot. It would be like closing your mind off. You have to be open to all types of information.

Along with curiosity came interest in continuous self-improvement. As Beth Stevenson observed, "I am always looking for other opportunities that are challenging; workshops, new information, and new projects. I feel like I am continuously evolving, so this allows for creativity and constant on-the-job learning." Alex Banful viewed learning as the lifeblood of his organization, both for himself and others.

> I have a voracious appetite for knowledge. Once I develop an interest in something, there is no stopping. I have a firm belief in the development of people; that has been the livewire of this organization. I pick people young and have molded all of them. I have not spared any expense in their development because most of our people participate in a lot of executive education in the U.S. Invariably, you find you are the sole person from Africa in the class, and that has been one of the motivators.

Consistent with CJ Nickerson's self-described creative bent, he made his own learning opportunities.

> At the state department, we would get one professional meeting a year. I would create my own conference throughout the state by scheduling meetings to get together with those who have a common interest. I'm not a good session attendee at a conference; [I would] rather have a cup of coffee with a colleague and a professional exchange. That contributed a lot to my professional growth.

When he became CEO of his own foundation, CJ encouraged others to find a learning approach that worked for them and to pursue it. Whether through conferences, readings, or more experientially based events, he promoted both opportunities and expectations for continuous learning.

Beyond cultivating and nurturing their own curiosity, most of the leaders attempted to instill a similar love of learning throughout their organizations. Rich Teerlink was disposed to do that at Harley-Davidson.

> I see myself as instinctually curious. I felt that most organizations spend too much time in training and not enough time on competence. We have a program called Awareness Expansion where we brought future leaders within the company to hear varying points of view—from Peter Senge to Peter Block— just to expand our ability to think about the world.

Nola was very direct in the way she attempted to instill productive habits in her organization.

> We teach critical thinking skills and encourage creativity here. I think it's part of my role that I cannot define. It's about giving opportunities, encouraging, nurturing, valuing. I've become more structured and strategic in my approach. I evaluate the learning opportunity. I will engage in it and encourage others to do the same.

INVESTED

The leaders were disposed to be centered, analytic, creative, positive, persistent, and curious. They were so disposed because they perceived that such habits of mind and behavior were of sustaining value to their leadership influence on the achievement of goals. Given their embrace of the described dispositions, it was a given that they would model and promote like habits in their organizations. Indeed, their reflections indicated that they did so, in many natural and informal ways, as they went about their leadership business. The leaders also promoted their dispositional bias more formally. That is, they were disposed to invest in developing productive habits throughout their organizations.

> "The thrill is in the learning, not the destination point. The fulfillment comes with the communal sense of achievement."
>
> — *Denese Henare*

Bob Knight's general approach to such investment was to continuously monitor what was transpiring within his organization and stay alert to educational opportunities.

> If you train people very, very well, they don't need to be so heavily maintained. If you don't train people well, you will continuously have troubles. So it's about constant training, constant training, constant training.

Bob also shared that, in the business realm, the CEO often has a certain goal in mind. By encouraging others through input and the exercise of creative problem solving along the path to the goal, both productivity and commitment increase.

> I may say we need to go to Z, and I think we should do A, B, and G. But they are the ones who are on the front line and are thinking about it all the time. So they may suggest a few different paths but still leading to Z. I reinforce their ideas because all I want is to get to Z. It may not have been what I had in mind, but they have input and own the idea. They will do everything possible to make sure it gets done, and often theirs is a better way.

As reported earlier, Nola Hambleton was very direct in her disposition to invest in the cultivation of productive thinking habits in her organization. Nola elaborated on this theme by observing that she was consciously attempting to nurture a positive disposition for creative problem solving in her teachers.

> I do the same [encourage creativity] now with teachers in a more strategic way. They put in a proposal. They have to tell me what the outcomes are. I have to see what the benefits are for the school first. There are times when a

teacher will come to me and say, "I really would like to try this." I'll say, "Okay, what are you going to do and why are you going to do it?" I think the teachers are getting better at it.

Frank Lukasavitz shared a similar interest in encouraging the creative problem-solving capacity of others.

> To energize students, I have them read a book called *The Five Rings*. It is a book about preparation . . . about a Japanese Samurai. It's about how to prepare yourself for life and how to solve problems. If you want to design something, I have my students think of five ways to do it . . . to think laterally.

Investing in the solution-seeking capacity of others was an articulated goal for most of the 36 leaders. CJ Nickerson described himself as a critical and creative problem solver who encouraged his employees to be the same. He did so because he generally believed in the value and importance of investing in others. He also did it for a very practical reason: because he knew it was necessary if the job was going to get done.

> When I look back on my career, I have consistently tried to convince the staff to be creative. I often found myself getting sucked back into the business side, so I tried to create the opportunity for others to do what I really wanted to be doing: to work more directly on health education.

Accordingly, CJ continually sought to encourage others to lead foundation efforts, which in turn helped many of his associates grow and move up in the organization. "I wanted them to see that their personal efforts would help CHEF be recognized for its leadership in the Northwest and nationally. They did a great job."

Likewise, Alex Banful worked to develop a sustaining solution-seeking mentality among his employees.

> I've gotten staff to think about running their programs as small businesses. They are writing business plans. I'm their donor, and they have to convince me that I want to keep their program funded. They work in teams and defend their programs. If your plan is great, you get it funded. The whole idea was to get a system of strategic thinking embedded in the organization. I'm not going to be here all of the time. You don't want an institution where the thinking is left for the manager to do and the others just to follow. I'm asking them to do the thinking themselves. I think the ownership of it becomes even stronger. They have to look 2 or 3 years down the road, how the whole thing is going to shape up and how they are going to run their program once it has been approved.

Through such nurturing of productive thinking and behavior in others, the leaders sought to systemically expand their leadership influence. Notably, they nurtured productive habits in their associates, knowing that such investment would likely lead to many leaving their organizations. Nola Hambleton saw her employees as bundles of potential that she had a responsibility to mentor and develop.

> My staff are enthusiastic young people. Most of them have leadership ability; that's why I chose them. So I expect that they are going to become school leaders. They need to have that background and understanding. I've been given these opportunities to see the big picture in education; I think they should know that too. They need to understand why we do things. If they understand the structure of the system, it's going to be easier for them.

Ian Fox shared a similar perspective.

> I think in the 16 years I've been here, I've had five deputy principals who are now leading their own schools as principals. Teachers don't leave the school just to do something similar at another school; they leave here to go to a leadership role. I'd rather lose a good deputy every few years than have a deputy who wanted to die here, I suppose.

The leaders' sense of systemic influence through investment in others was not so much the product of formal training as intuitive understanding of the mechanisms needed to sustain efforts that they initiated and valued. Alex Banful demonstrated this intuition in commenting on his compulsion to cultivate responsibility in himself and others.

> One of the things that drives me is the need to be responsible to yourself so you can be responsible for yourself. Because of this, I try to help others develop the ability to be responsible to themselves so that, ultimately, they can be responsible for themselves.

A classic Chinese quotation hanging in Rod Chamberlain's office was also representative of this perception.

> When the leader governs, the people are barely aware that he exists.
>
> Next best is a leader who is loved.
>
> Next, one who is feared.
>
> Next, one who is despised.
>
> If you don't trust the people, you will make them untrustworthy.
>
> The leader doesn't talk, he acts.
>
> When his work is done, the people say, "Amazing, we did it all by ourselves."
>
> *—Toa Te Ching, 17*

Lessons Learned

The concept of sustainability is perhaps best understood within a broad context. For example, a popular definition of sustainability that emerged from a 1987 UN conference defined sustainable elements and activities as those that respond to present needs without compromising the ability of future generations to meet their needs. This perspective is often presented as a version of the golden rule, that is, "Do unto future generations as you would have them do onto you" (Gilman, 1990). Beyond sustaining their personal will and energy, then, the interviewed leaders were equally concerned, if not more so, with prolonging the positive effects of their leadership influence on the future achievements of their organizations and generations to come.

STEPPING UP TO SUSTAINABILITY

The 36 leaders were disposed to sustain their influence on others toward the achievement of meaningful purpose by being *centered, analytic, creative, positive, persistent, curious,* and *invested.* This was what they perceived the essence of their leadership character and behavior to be and how they aspired to having an enduring effect on the culture of their organization. Productive dispositions in thinking and behavior were, in effect, the means by which the leaders moved beyond leadership of the moment and "stepped up" to sustainable leadership (see Figure 8.1).

> "What we have here is a culture of professionalism, excellence, and results—combined with a lot of hard work."
>
> —Alex Banful

Ultimately, the leaders aspired to promote a cultural disposition to get the job done and done well. Out of both a desire to develop more effective systems centered on their vision of important purpose and a sincere value for growing leadership from within, the leaders worked to promote productive habits of thinking and behavior throughout their organizations. They were not interested in quick fixes or easy answers; rather, they were centered on a direction and purpose for the long haul. They were also disposed to the exercise of analytic and creative thinking to produce meaningful changes and resolutions within that purpose. Their interactions with members of their organizations encouraged the exploration of new perspectives and reflection about what could be rather than what was.

The leaders were further disposed to be both positive and persistent in their efforts to either initiate or reform the organizations as required to achieve their purpose. It would not be unflattering to suggest that they conveyed a stubborn focus on purpose augmented by a strong work ethic. And within that ethic, they were disposed to be curious in their embrace of new knowledge and

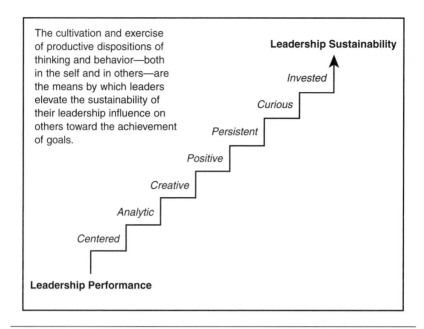

The cultivation and exercise of productive dispositions of thinking and behavior—both in the self and in others—are the means by which leaders elevate the sustainability of their leadership influence on others toward the achievement of goals.

Leadership Sustainability

Invested

Curious

Persistent

Positive

Creative

Analytic

Centered

Leadership Performance

Figure 8.1   The Elevation of Leadership Influence Through Sustaining Dispositions

challenges and to invest in others through the cultivation of similar disposi-tions. Significantly, the leaders observed that they nurtured the dissemination of all of their dispositional traits, in some manner, within their organizational cultures. As they saw it, the key to sustaining their leadership was to create organizations populated by people who could do without them. Such an ori-entation to leadership again demonstrated the leaders' humility and commit-ment to service.

EXTENDING COHERENCE

As described in previous chapters, the base of inner coherence about values and commitment forged by leadership formation was subsequently extended to a broader coherence that incor-porated congruent leadership performance—in both character and behavior. In this chapter, we observe the further extension of leadership coherence by sustaining dispo-sitions that both expand and compound leadership influence (see Figure 8.2). It is an

> "My goal is to enable people to take control of their own lives so they can contribute to the fullfillment of other lives."
>
> —*Tim Brighouse*

extension that most immediately arises from the prominent character traits and behaviors within leadership performance aligned to human capacity, as described in Chapters 4 through 7. It is an extension that is also traceable, moreover, to core values that give rise to congruent leadership performance.

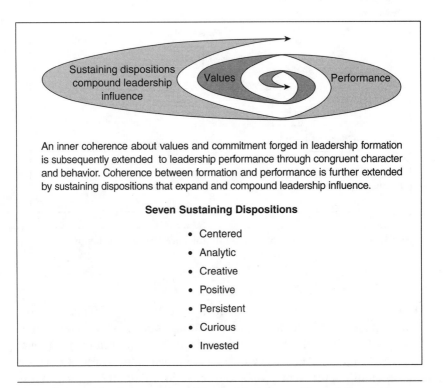

An inner coherence about values and commitment forged in leadership formation is subsequently extended to leadership performance through congruent character and behavior. Coherence between formation and performance is further extended by sustaining dispositions that expand and compound leadership influence.

Seven Sustaining Dispositions

- Centered
- Analytic
- Creative
- Positive
- Persistent
- Curious
- Invested

Figure 8.2   The Compounding of Leadership Influence Through Sustaining Dispositions

Thus, the major components of coherent leadership become visible in the form of a spiral model. It is a model that portrays natural and logical connections between values, congruent character and behavior, and sustaining dispositions; that is, a model of coherent leadership formation, performance, and sustainability.

There is another piece of the sustainability picture, however, yet to be addressed. That piece presents insights the interviewed leaders shared about their strategies for maintaining personal viability and endurance within leadership roles that were physically, mentally, and emotionally demanding. Accordingly, our conversation next addresses the sustaining strategies that the leaders employed to maintain themselves—strategies that sustained the leader behind the leadership so that the consequence of his or her influence might be fully realized. But before we move on, take time to reflect for a few minutes about your experience with sustaining leadership dispositions, as facilitated by the concluding section of this chapter.

Further Conversation

The focus of your leadership reflection at this time, as facilitated by Exercise 8.1, is about personal dispositions, the origin of dispositions, the effect of dispositions, and the cultivation of dispositions in the self and others. (Again, this can be conducted either individually or in the company of colleagues, as you prefer.)

EXERCISE 8.1   Further Conversation: Sustaining
Leadership Dispositions

A. What dispositions (i.e., habits, tendencies, inclinations) best define you as a leader?

B. What are the origins of your dispositions (i.e., where do they come from)?

C. How do your leadership dispositions sustain (i.e., maintain) your leadership influence?

D. How do you cultivate productive dispositions

In yourself?

In others?

9

Sustaining Strategies

I have taken a moment here to rest, to steal a view of the glorious vista that surrounds me, to look back on the distance I have come. But I can rest only for a moment, for with freedom come responsibilities, and I dare not linger, for my long walk is not yet ended.

—Mandela (1995, p. 751)

Sustaining Self

Leadership can be a lonely and exhausting enterprise. Leaders are often one of a kind in their organizations and, as we might observe from the unfolding of this leadership conversation, inclined to take their work very seriously. Working long hours and bearing huge responsibilities, leaders must routinely call on inner reserves of strength and commitment to maintain their effectiveness.

As observed through the stories shared by the 36 leaders thus far, leadership was not a path that they chose for purposes of self-aggrandizement and individual reward. Their self-described values and character consistently spoke to sincere humility and a strong service orientation. As they saw it, their interest in sustaining their leadership influence emanated first and foremost from commitment to purpose rather than ego. From that perspective, the defining dispositions of being centered, analytic, creative, positive, persistent, curious, and invested (as described in Chapter 8) arose from their mission.

The good news is that there was a bonus to be realized from such a strong dispositional orientation to compelling purpose. That is, the dispositions that served a sustained leadership influence on the pursuit of organizational purpose also helped sustain the leader behind the leadership. The same dispositions that promoted an enduring influence on purpose also helped the leaders remain centered, analytic, creative, positive, persistent, curious, and invested on a personal level.

Helpful as this win-win effect was, however, the leaders were nevertheless human beings, and they were very aware of further need for sustaining their capacity to carry on and continue the good fight.

What emerged from the conversations with the interviewed leaders was an understanding that leaders must proactively insure personal longevity of practice and, thereby, the long-term viability of their potential for achieving desired results. Awareness of this need was not always enough, however, as taking care of oneself was sometimes a hard-learned lesson. In a few cases, the hard work that they demanded of themselves and the high expectations that they set led to physical problems along the way. But whether by necessity or through foresight, they all eventually came to the conclusion that if their commitment to their life's work was important, then so was their commitment to their health and longevity as leaders. Accordingly, seven strategies for maintaining self emerged as being particularly worthy of their leadership attention.

Seven Significant Strategies

The 36 leaders were consciously aware of the importance of attending to their personal welfare and offered many insights about how they attempted to nurture mind, body, and soul. The seven prominent strategies that emerged from their collective reflections indicate that a leader is well advised to stay fit, manage emotion, value counsel, create space, get charged, seek stimulation, and welcome inspiration.

STAY FIT

As many of us have experienced, taking care of the body has a payoff for the mind, resulting in mental alertness, heightened energy, and lowered stress. Although they are frequently encouraged to pursue such results, leaders are no different than the rest of us in often being slow to take heed of the good advice. Many of the interviewed leaders, however, stepped up to the challenge because they understood and appreciated the benefits to their leadership performance. Ross Gilbert was very dedicated to his physical well-being.

> "You have to take care of yourself. If you don't, then you can't work in the way that I have defined this job."
>
> — *Roger Harmon*

I'm good to myself. If I'm tired during the day, I'll have a little nap. If I have a 15-minute nap, then I'm ready for work. I exercise a lot. I swim three to four times a week. My wife and I walk a lot—bush walks and bird watching. We eat very carefully most of the time. I also drink wine and it nurtures me, especially good wine. I spend time with my grandchild. Every Wednesday afternoon, I take her out in the park and push her around in her stroller. This is lovely, very nurturing to me and to her, I guess. We have a good social life at home. I'm very good about looking after myself.

Mandy Macleod used physical activity as a way to distance herself from work.

I play sports: tennis, golf, go to the gym, get out in the fresh air. I have the ability to switch off. I can go home and put it behind me and do other things. I have a place where I can relax in my home.

While Julianne Lowe wasn't as successful at separating body care from an active mind, she nevertheless tried.

I go for a massage. It doesn't stop my mind, but it does take care of my body. You have to look after yourself physically and give your mind a rest. I sleep really well, and that's a huge advantage. I've always been a good sleeper unless something is really serious. I can usually let go of the everyday stuff.

Engaging in physical activity and avoiding bringing work and stress home was a priority for Boon Yoon Chiang.

I try to exercise, and I try not to bring work home. I think it is important to try to have more for your family life. If you bring your work home, I don't think that is healthy. I try to play golf at least once a week, and I do a lot of walking. I think the key thing is to keep yourself healthy.

Another business leader, Bob Knight, used exercise for his physical well-being and as a means to spend quality time with his wife. "We get up every morning at 5 A.M., 5 days a week, and take a brisk 2-mile walk. I really enjoy our time together."

Jeanne Dukes was one of the leaders who had learned lessons about the value of maintaining physical health the hard way.

A year ago, I went to a doctor and my whole body was falling apart. I started taking medication and started walking. I walk 5 days a week at 5:30 . . . up and down the hill we live on. It's making a big difference. My husband goes with me and that helps. I have more energy, and I don't eat as much bad stuff. I've managed to move my focus from what I am going to eat to managing my day.

Often, the leaders were searching for or had found a more holistic approach. Roger Harmon was one leader who had done so.

I learned how to do Qi Gong in the park. Every morning, I do Qui Gong, sometimes not in a serious or formal or even a meditative way. It really lets the energy flow. That is probably the most important thing I do for myself, physically and emotionally.

A few of the leaders were still struggling with the concept of fitness, though they knew that it was something that needed their attention. CJ Nickerson had a 50-mile commute to work every morning and evening. He used his travel time for reflection, but exercise was often neglected.

> I tried to have walk-and-talk meetings to get some exercise, and on the way home I tried to process the day so I wouldn't have to bring the garbage home, but it was difficult. When I left, I was in the worst physical shape I had ever been. Work was just too all consuming. I couldn't get away from it. Others may be smarter than I was, but I couldn't get away from it.

The point made over and over, nevertheless, was that staying fit was essential. Even a leader as busy as Helen Clark, Prime Minister of New Zealand, could do something about making time for fitness. She was committed to going home on the weekends and regularly exercising and watching her diet. Most notably, she engaged in frequent mountain-climbing expeditions.

MANAGE EMOTION

As we observed earlier, a critical component within the formation experience of the interviewed leaders was surviving adversity in their youth or early adulthood. With such reference to their self-efficacy and ability to survive and thrive during tough times, they appreciated and cultivated their capacity to deal with the emotional load of leadership. The ability to keep an emotional distance was observed by Rod Chamberlain.

> "I don't get stressed as such. I just get focused."
>
> —Ian Fox

> I have the ability to put things behind me and move on. Reflection can digress into obsessive behavior. At points, I have to say, I have gotten lessons out of this and I need to let go of it. I think that is hard because you think about your virtues and your vices, and if you are reflective, you can get stuck. I have watched too many people get stuck, and I also know that I cannot achieve my mission if I get stuck. It's one thing to sit back and reflect; it's another to get stuck.

As a female in a leadership role, Mandy Macleod paid particular attention to the control of her emotions.

> I am very even tempered on the surface. I think it is very much something you have to [have] when you deal with people. They need to see calmness; they don't want to see you losing your temper. They don't want to see you dissolving into tears, and if you have a tendency to do these things, and I'm not giving any secrets away, you do it in private. I think the face of an administrator

can oftentimes be very different from what I really feel on the inside. I have enormous temper tantrums at home, but not here.

Another female leader, Julianne Lowe, cultivated a very purposeful method to deal with her feelings.

When I get angry about something, I ask why. Am I angry with the other person, or am I angry with myself for not getting it right? I've learned not to be such a hard taskmaster for myself. I have gotten comfortable in my skin.

Learning when to say yes and when to say no was another strategy used to keep a healthy emotional plane. Ian Fox described his intention to do so.

I'm quite selective about the things I do now. I go to the things I think I should support. I think I've learned to be good at prioritizing. I monitor my own time quite well in terms of what I am able to achieve. I've certainly learned the art of delegation over the years. I think I've certainly done that for others, and they've moved on into their own leadership positions.

Mechai Viraviayda found that an effective way to manage tremendous daily stressors was to keep work in perspective. He commented, "Stress is not a problem for me. It goes back to my belief that most of life is challenge, so it becomes normal. The best thing to do is try to forget it. Generally, I'm not stressed." Patrick Sayne adopted a similar outlook.

I will do what I can and then I let it go. You have to be able to let it go or you'll tie yourself into a knot. Whatever happens happens. You also have to choose your battles and know when to walk away and know when you are just going to lose. Sometimes you pursue [it] for the symbolism. There is a certain amount of saying, "This is a game" or "It doesn't really matter" because there are other things you have to do. You need to know the difference between what is and isn't central to your core values. In the end, it really doesn't matter. The world is not going to rise or fall on something that happened to me. As long as there is a teacher to meet those students in the morning, not a hell of a lot can happen that is really bad. You don't want to give up, but there is always another day.

Understanding that she does the best she can at any given time and place, Julianne Lowe noted the power of letting go.

Emotionally, I try to keep my distance. I distance myself and know that there is only so much that I can do. There is no fault in whatever I have done because whatever I have done I have done to the best of my ability and can't do any more. I have learned to accept that I'm not perfect. I pushed myself really hard for years in everything. When my shop failed, I had to take stock as a single parent. I felt inadequate because there was only me. When it failed, it made me accept my limitations. It's wonderful getting older because you have to see things in yourself and it's okay. . . . You don't have to be perfect every day. You realize that you are not superwoman and can't be perfect at everything. I'm doing the best that I can.

Richard Bissen added description of a certain mental toughness that lives concurrently with a mental softness, something he saw as a comfortable paradox.

I am the youngest in my family, but most people think I am the oldest. We all have pretty strong and independent personalities. We call that our Nokoa side, which is the warrior from my mom's side of the family. I take my job seriously, but not myself seriously. I'm really two different people. People who know me outside of work see me playing music, telling stories and jokes. Then people will see me working here and say, "I didn't know you were so serious," and vice versa. I can be intense, but mostly I'm laid back.

VALUE COUNSEL

The interviewed leaders were well aware of the need for establishing and maintaining strong social bonds for themselves, even as they nurtured them in others. They found that a sense of connectedness was necessary to combat isolation, so trusted sounding boards were actively sought. Having a tight inner circle of social support, whether family or friends, was a universal need that all of these leaders addressed.

> "You learn that your best friend, and probably your only true friend, is your spouse."
>
> — Kuami Pianim

Spouses and children were often mentioned as the backbone of the social support structure, as Brenda Schoonover described.

I bounce ideas off of my husband . . . use him as a sounding board. He's had 32 years of experience in the Foreign Service, and that has been very helpful. I also try to get feedback from people, as I get to know people here. I bounce ideas off of my office management assistant because she knows me very well. I went for 2½ months with six people in that job until she came. I think having people you trust that you can bounce things off of is essential.

Gary Rasmussen agreed that support of a life partner was precious.

I have a spouse who is a great influence and can give me vital feedback through different lenses than I am emotionally experiencing. Anyone that has a partner who is willing to give of that time is so fortunate.

Trusted friends, often outside the work environment, offered a safe haven for blowing off steam or seeking advice. Mandy Macleod described a group of people that were indispensable to her.

I have a group of friends from outside of school, from the sports club and from taking Spanish lessons. They have no connection to the school, and I think that really has helped. My social life is, of course, part of school because you go to everything. You are expected to go to everything, which is fine because you want to be there . . . but I think it is really great that I can go home on the weekend and I'm not looking to school for my social life. I think you can be too easily overwhelmed by the work. I also have a very good colleague who administers in another school in another county, and I see her from time to time. We have a wonderful evening together where we really groan and moan. I think it's called a "bitch session." She and I are each other's safe sounding boards. I think you lose credibility if you have one person, particularly on the staff, that you confide in. I think that's really divisive. I think you really have to treat everybody exactly the same and not have favorites. You're very isolated in a job like this. You're part of the staff, but very much not part of the staff. To single one person out as confidant is a disaster.

Bob Knight agreed with the need for such support outside the workplace.

I engage in outside activities with friends who are outside of the company. I think it's important to keep a little distance from the employees so that you can make the hard decisions when you need to. On the other hand, I think it's important to have good people around you at work that you can trust and talk to. I don't try to be perfect.

Occasionally, internal advisors who were in leadership roles were called on if trusted completely. Superintendent Patrick Sayne relied on fellow administrators.

I use my assistant superintendent and other people I trust as a sounding board. I ask them if I was off base. Generally, they will tell me. I use other superintendents once you get beyond the ego and the posturing. One of the issues of leadership is thinking you have to appear invulnerable. It is difficult to shed that in front of your colleagues. But with those I trust, they will tell me if I am acting like a horse's ass. I know they will support me even though they may try to correct my behavior.

Similarly, Michael Barber found internal advisors indispensable to his high-pressure role as advisor to the prime minister. For him, such relationships were cultivated and maintained over time.

Two of the people who work here have worked for me all through the last 5 years and at the university before that. Each time I've gotten a new job, I've insisted that they come with me because it's really important to have people who are friends and completely trustworthy. There are lots of times when reforms were falling apart, and having people who sustain you as a human being was really important.

An ongoing challenge for many was finding the balance between home, work, and friends. Michael Barber also expressed gratitude for the support his family provided.

> I have three daughters and a wonderful wife and friend. The most difficult times to work are if you are worrying about one of them. Making sure that those relationships are valued throughout and in spite of being driven, that you don't lose the focus [on family]. . . . That's important. We've done well, but they've been patient and good.

For Gabor Halmai, finding balance was a hard-learned lesson. As with many leaders, the second time around proved more successful.

> It is interesting because these challenges were at the same time as the challenges in my private life. I have tried to change my private life and not make the same mistakes as I did in my previous marriage. For instance, what I never could have imagined before, I was invited to Indonesia, and I'm flying on Sunday for a 1-day conference. I decided why don't we go for a holiday. I invited my wife and we're going to spend 2 weeks. I'd never imagined that I'd let go for 2 weeks.

CREATE SPACE

Time to think, time to be alone, time to get away. The 36 leaders were well aware of the need for such precious commodities and took action to assure that they had both the time and the mental and physical space to reflect on their work. Sometimes, as Rod Chamberlain observed, just having the mental discipline to create such space produced immediate benefits.

> "I love climbing mountains whenever I get the chance. That's when I clear the air."
>
> —Michael Barber

> One of the things that I have gotten better at is taking time to reflect and think. I am a product of a Germanic culture where reflection time is not seen as productive. So I intentionally take the time to go out on our deck overlooking a dairy and creek in Wisconsin or the sugar cane fields here. This helps me to think about what I am doing and how am I doing and what more I can be doing.

Taking the time and advantage of existing space worked for Ross Gilbert, whose office abutted the Sydney Botanical Gardens.

> I sit over there with a book I want to read, and I look out the window at the gardens. I just change my space in the office and sit and reflect. Sometimes I put away my reading and reflect in my diary [calendar] on the days' activities. I think about them and what I am going to do and how I am going to carry through my basic principle of action during the day.

Sometimes a tool was needed to assist the unwinding process. Golf was the tool of choice for Boon Yoon Chiang.

> I took up golf and I don't play that well, but I enjoy it. I used to play competitive tennis at one point in time, but golf is different. You have to relax first before you play. If your mind is occupied with a lot, you don't play well. I learned to forget everything else when I play. I think that helps in a way to put aside problems you have in the office. If you bring it home, it might have an impact on your relationship with your family. I don't think that is the right way to do it.

Gary Rasmussen found that the leadership context impacted his ability to find both time and space.

> Hong Kong accelerates the pace so much more here. In the business community, people are used to doing things overnight, whereas in the United States, you go through all kinds of laws and things. Things happen quickly here, so you have to be able to respond quickly, taking away some of your own time to reflect. There has to be a physical separation in a different setting. For me, it's getting out of the house and going for a walk. I walk for an hour, hour and a half, and during that time I can cover a lot of topics.

Margo Dévai talked about the need for physical separation as well and the need to set boundaries on her accessibility.

> I don't like company because I meet so many people. I would like to have alone time. It doesn't happen very often. I am planning to have more time for the things that I like. I need it. I'm trying to set limits on my time now. I have to preserve some time just for myself because otherwise I wouldn't be able to put out the same results on a high level.

Hobbies were a means that Mandy Macleod used to create time and an emotional outlet.

> I'm very interested in antiques, so I go marketing on a Sunday afternoon with a friend who has never been to my school, and I think that is really an important thing. When it's holiday time, I read rubbish, the trashier the better. During the school term, I read professionally and during holidays, I read the most god-awful garbage and it is wonderful. It's complete escapism. I think it is really important. I can escape in music. If I'm having a really bad day, I go home and listen to Andrea Bocelli, and it takes the sting out of the day.

Likewise, Roger Harmon cultivated a pastime that took him away from the worries of Peace Corps administration. "Photography is very important; sketching and flower arranging sometimes too . . . the creative part." As Donald Gwira put it, "I like to play. I bring out the child in me. Never let the child in you die."

Beth Stevenson suggested that sensing and responding to the need to get away can be either premeditated or spontaneous. " Every once in a while, I bust out to do something that feels personal to me, like backpacking in the Grand Canyon or the Appalachian Trail . . . putting myself on the edge." On the other hand, Julianne Lowe built time and space into her daily routines.

> I remember when I was nursing, the tutor sister said that to be a good nurse you have to have outside interests. I think that applies to any intense job. I make sure, even when I am away in hotels and motels, I go to movies. I read and belong to a book club. I will take a walk if my body feels really tense. . . . [I will] do things that are totally outside my job.

Michael Barber found a daily routine that helped him as well. "I cycle to and from work every day. I shower when I get here and change into work clothes. So that's a really nice part of my day, and I reflect as I cycle back and forth."

Christine Rodriguez discovered that it was necessary to take time for herself and was just as adamant that her colleagues did so as well.

> I work very hard to balance my life. Without that balance, you do get burned out. I tell my team that they need to take their scheduled vacations and not check in all the time. I do this. I travel around the world and don't take my laptop. I need to reenergize and create space. It's really true that when you do take that time off, you get more creative.

GET CHARGED

The interviewed leaders were energized by progress toward their compelling purpose. In effect, they were "charged" by the successful results of their leadership efforts. Because they had developed strong constructs about what they wanted to accomplish and clear visions for what success looked like, they found energy in both the journey and the destination. As Ross Gilbert noted, "It's a good day if I feel that I have motivated my students to think and do and be interested in something that they hadn't previously been interested in. I like that."

Michael Barber was very clear in his mind that his passion lifted the workload he carried and that the achieved results provided him the energy he needed to continue.

> "It's not money that drives me, but people. It's the little things that bring such complete change in their lives. It feels good when you can help make that change. For me, it's a religion."
>
> —Alex Banful

> I'm very committed to the ultimate goals, safe communities, children learning. I've talked a lot about systems, but if they weren't leading to outcomes that I believe are important and could get very emotional and passionate

about, then I wouldn't do them with the same obsession as the ultimate goal. It's not even the children passing the test; it's the child being able to read and write well. The fact that I know that as a result of those programs, 16,000 more children achieved that standard than 4 years ago, and we've made the fastest progress in the most disadvantaged parts of the country, that's what makes it all worthwhile. There is a huge degree of emotion and that goes back to what we talked about . . . my parents believing you should make a difference.

Having a deeply rooted belief system that was operationalized at work was a source of strength that Richard Bissen depended on.

The only people that come here are people who have been hurt. I used to think that the world was made up of two kinds of people: people who have been hurt and people who have done the hurting. That's all we would see every day. Of course the work is made up of much more than that. But I believe in the power of the truth and correcting the wrongs. It's all you can do. . . . It's all you can do. I go home to three kids every day. They have to live in this society. So even if it is someone else's child that was hurt, it could have been mine.

As Margo Dévai expressed it, not only did compelling purpose provide energy, but it also eliminated any possibility of not moving ahead.

The first source of energy is my goals. They are given by life. For example, last year there was a big grant application and we couldn't apply for it; only schools could. And they could choose us. The Minister of Education was behind it, so it was a very big thing. It gave me energy to achieve this. As a result, we had many trainings at the same time at different parts of the country. The energy is given by the fact that you have to do it.

The sheer joy of seeing intended results for students and teachers unfold fueled Rod Chamberlain's ongoing commitment.

It's a joy to see how many things I can influence and in the end, they will say, "We worked this out pretty well." Ten years ago, I found a book called *The On-Purpose Person.* The author [Kevin W. McCarthy] uses a metaphor of a light switch. Our purpose is either on or off. It describes a man who is very successful on the outside but going crazy on the inside. I take the time to be sure about where I am going and how I will get there.

Staying connected to those with whom he worked and intended to serve was important to energizing Roger Harmon's ongoing focus on purpose.

The most useful thing I do is to be with volunteers. They are the primary reason I came . . . to support and mentor their experience. The closer I get to their experience, the more affirmed I am, the more it means to me. If I go too long without being in immediate contact with volunteers, there's something wrong.

Because of the daily distractions of leadership, Tim Brighouse also found it important to reconnect to purpose and become rejuvenated on a regular basis.

> I find being in school and teaching kids renews me. I may be physically tired but intellectually and spiritually charged. To them it may be boringly obvious, and to me it is suddenly bringing into sharp focus something that I didn't even remember. [I feel like] I'm doing something; it's people, ideas, and being in school.

Rather than becoming overwhelmed by the magnitude of his calling, Mechai was motivated by it: "There are 10 million people in Thailand who make less than a dollar a day. If we can help those people, that is something worthwhile." Rich Teerlink was also driven by a need to feel a personal connection to the people he served.

> In 1983, we laid off 40% of our people at Harley-Davidson. I vowed we would never do that again. These are not faceless people. They have families, and we can have a traumatic impact on them. We have a responsibility to them. In my mind, the responsibility to them is greater than the responsibility to the stakeholders. If we serve them well, in all probability we will succeed. I am sustained by the fact that we are an economic entity, and adding value to all those who participate keeps me going.

Nola Hambleton perhaps best summed up the importance of connecting to and getting charged by what is most important: "The day I get up and don't want to come to school is the day that I'm finished. My heart belongs in a school."

SEEK STIMULATION

The 36 leaders never communicated satisfaction with their current level of learning and understanding. They routinely sought out mental stimulation from new ideas and information to keep their own intellectual networks growing and flowing. Boon Yoon Chiang turned to reading for such stimulation.

> "I love to read. I like literature. It gives me energy and refreshes my mind."
>
> —*Margo Dévai*

> I read a lot—books on all things—because as a [former] journalist, I have widened my interests. So I read on all sorts of things, just for the fun of it. It keeps me abreast of what is happening in other fields apart from what I am doing. Hopefully, that will help me to manage myself better.

Similarly, Rod Chamberlain read widely and purposefully explored ideas that were outside of his field of education.

> I subscribe to the *FAST Journal*. I also go to conferences to network and see what others are thinking and doing, more than the canned speeches. The conversations are more engaging. It's more my learning style. I'm a very visual person, and when I get confused, I start to draw diagrams and chart out the information. We see how messy and chaotic it is at first, and then we begin to make sense of it.

Many of the leaders sought intellectual stimulation in the company of others. Gary Rasmussen sought professional affiliation through community involvement.

> I've been involved in Rotary. I was supposed to be president, but I declined. I just didn't have the time, but I represent Interact to our students. Here, we have 160 kids that are involved in Rotary Interact and community service. That charges my batteries . . . direct contact with kids in schools.

Jeanne Dukes relied on multiple interactions with colleagues to stimulate her thinking.

> I form relationships to find out about things. I like to keep contacts with people who know about a variety of things. My processing and theorizing is people based, not thing based. I want to know what other people know and think about. People are endlessly fascinating to me . . . so if they want to tell me, I will listen.

In response to the ever-changing workplace, Bob Knight regularly engaged in ongoing learning, to help him adapt.

> I take classes to regenerate, to get a fresh perspective, or to validate what I already do. It's always good to learn new lessons because this is a new generation of employees, so that you need a matching perspective.

Denese Henare summed up the attraction of the regular infusion of new knowledge in expressing a sentiment widely shared among the interviewed leaders: "I love the thrill of learning. There's no final destination point."

WELCOME INSPIRATION

Although spiritual orientations and matters of faith were not specifically addressed in the interview protocol, a connection to a greater force or a sense of oneness or unity with the universe was important to most of the leaders. Seeing themselves as a tool in some grand design, or part of a larger scheme to

> "'What does the Lord require of you but to do justice and to love kindness and to walk humbly with your God.' Yes, that's it."
>
> —*Ross Gilbert*

direct and advance the lot of humankind, mattered. Such perspective accented their purpose and provided sustaining drive for their leadership. Julianne Lowes's faith was an example of such effect.

Being a Baha'i helps. I found something that is consistent with my values. When you look and accept that there are some things you can't deal with, and you can turn it over to God, it levels me and puts me back into balance. Before I was a Baha'i, it was more confusing. It puts things more in perspective and puts the missing pieces in place. There is goodness in all of us. Mankind is one. It doesn't matter what age, color, or culture. We are all human beings with the same fears and the same emotions, and there is goodness in all of us that needs to be nurtured.

Forming a consistent internal schema for beliefs and reflection was essential for Michael Barber.

I really appreciate, benefit from, and try to live by the values and attitudes I learned from my Quaker heritage. The Quaker phrase is that "There is God in every man." I apply the values of my upbringing regularly: patience, conflict resolution, value for others. In a Quaker meeting there are no priests; there is nobody who interprets the word of God. It is the relationship between you and God. You learn the power of listening to one another and you also learn to reflect on yourself.

A sense of accountability outside self that was also aligned with internal values kept Rod Chamberlain going.

My background is Mennonite, and there is accountability to the community. I'm a participating member of a church congregation. This gives me a group of people that have the same values that I have. It's not about the exact details of the theology, but generally the same values.

Maori culture and spirituality fed Denese Henare in a similar manner: "I go back home and participate in the Maori environment to sustain my spiritual development. That renews me." Beth Stevenson explained a similar connection to her own leadership: " I have a calling as a lay minister and involve myself in pastoral care. It is high touch and helps to sustain me."

Kuami Pianim suggested that a faith connection builds a stronger leader.

Having a bit of faith helps. If God wants me to die, I'll die. When I went to prison, I was very frightened, very scared, but later I wasn't afraid to die.

> When you are not afraid to die, you are very dangerous because nobody can push you into a corner. You need inner strength to sustain you.

The 36 leaders might have subscribed to humility as individuals, but such posture did not negate lofty goals. Driven by their faith in a greater design or higher purpose both propelled and sustained their personal capacity for difficult and challenging leadership responsibilities. Rich Teerlink testified to his affinity for significant impact.

> My goal is to change the world's view of leadership. I talk to groups and serve on boards to do so. I think the world can be a better place and anything we can do to help, we should.

Lessons Learned

At 65, Tim Brighouse was a picture of long-sustained leadership. He chuckled as he created metaphors for his remaining years as leader.

> Did you ever see the British marathoner, Jim Peters, who nearly won? He was an amazing runner, staggering towards the finish line with three people around him trying to help him through the line. I often say I'm at the Jim Peters stage of my career. The last 5 years I haven't taken much time to sit still. I used to have a car that was so bad at starting, I used to fill it up with gas, and I wouldn't turn the engine off because I thought it wouldn't start again. It's a bit like that, which is, oh my God, if I stop for a week, will I ever get the engine going?

> "You don't die of hard work, but you might die because you are unhappy or frustrated with your work. . . . You have to relax and control your emotions."
>
> —*Fanny Law*

Still motivated, energetic, and committed, it would take nothing short of forced retirement to remove Tim Brighouse from his superintendency. Typical of the interviewed leaders, he was already seeking out the next avenue for carrying on his passion for student success in the Birmingham District. Given such orientation to staying the course, the leaders did whatever it took to keep them viable. They did so by staying fit, managing emotion, valuing counsel, creating personal space, getting charged by results, seeking intellectual stimulation, and welcoming inspiration from a higher purpose. Figure 9.1 summarizes how such strategies sustained the personal capacity of the leader behind the leadership.

The lesson learned about leadership sustainability, then, is one of sustaining dispositions and strategies that together elevate leadership to

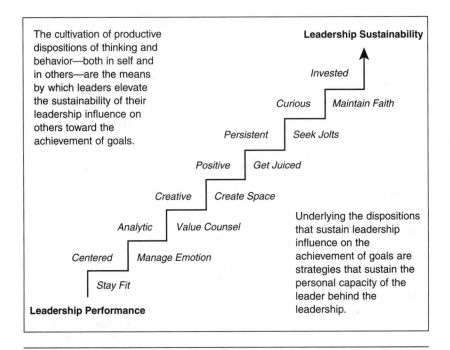

The cultivation of productive dispositions of thinking and behavior—both in self and in others—are the means by which leaders elevate the sustainability of their leadership influence on others toward the achievement of goals.

Leadership Sustainability

Invested

Curious   *Maintain Faith*

Persistent   *Seek Jolts*

Positive   *Get Juiced*

Creative   *Create Space*

Analytic   *Value Counsel*

Underlying the dispositions that sustain leadership influence on the achievement of goals are strategies that sustain the personal capacity of the leader behind the leadership.

Centered   *Manage Emotion*

Stay Fit

Leadership Performance

Figure 9.1   The Elevation of Leadership Through Sustaining Dispositions and Strategies

enduring influence and legacy. We can now observe yet a greater distinction of coherent leadership. An inner coherence about values forged in leadership formation is subsequently extended to a broader coherence with leadership performance. Leadership coherence is then further extended through sustaining dispositions that compound leadership influence. The dispositions that sustain leadership are, in turn, supported by strategies that sustain the personal capacity of the leader behind the leadership (see Figure 9.2).

With reference to the reflections of 36 leaders, rejoin the conversation through Further Conversation Exercise 9.1 to assess how you sustain yourself as the leader behind your leadership role (again, either individually or with colleagues, as you prefer).

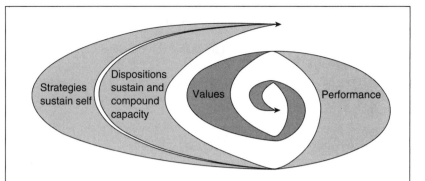

An inner coherence about values and commitment forged in leadership formation is subsequently extended to leadership performance through congruent character and behavior. Coherence between formation and performance is further extended by sustaining dispositions that expand and compound leadership influence. Underlying those dispositions are strategies that sustain the leader behind the leadership.

<table>
<tr><td colspan="2"></td></tr>
</table>

Seven Sustaining Dispositions	**Seven Sustaining Strategies**
• Centered	• Stay fit
• Analytic	• Manage emotion
• Creative	• Value counsel
• Positive	• Create space
• Persistent	• Get charged
• Curious	• Seek stimulation
• Invested	• Welcome inspiration

Figure 9.2   Compounding Leadership Through Sustaining Dispositions and Strategies

EXERCISE 9.1   Further Conversation: Sustaining Leadership Strategies

A. How do you endure the stress and strain that you encounter in your leadership role?

B. How do you nurture your personal welfare?

   Physically?

   Emotionally?

   Socially?

   Intellectually?

   Spiritually?

C. What spiritual or greater moral purpose, if any, do you associate with your leadership work, and how does that orientation affect you?

D. What results do you realize when you extend time and effort toward self-care?

E. What results do you realize when you do not extend time and effort toward self-care?

Part IV

Leadership Learned

> *One can take inspiration from those individuals who have not accepted the conventional wisdom, who have risked defeat, rejection, and obscurity in order to pursue ideas in which they (and perhaps a few followers) believe.*
>
> —Gardner (1995, p. xii)

C oherent leadership can be understood as a natural, logical, and dynamic alignment of leadership formation, performance, and sustainability. The culminating effect of such alignment is an expanded consequence of leadership influence—a leadership legacy.

10

A Coherent Story

Traditional conceptions of leadership tend to be so dominated by images of presidents and prime ministers speaking to the masses from on high that we may forget that the vast preponderance of personal influence is exerted quietly and subtly in everyday relationships.

—Burns (1978, p. 442)

The Bottom Line

Interviews with 36 leaders harvested 36 stories, many valuable insights, and four important themes.

Through conversations reaching across five continents, a diverse group of accomplished individuals offered up reflective insights about leadership formation, performance, and sustainability. The preceding nine chapters have profiled the storytellers and salient patterns of insight within those reflections. From those accounts, we can further interpret essential wisdom—the collective bottom line if you will—about what 36 leaders saw as important to consequential leadership influence on the achievement of meaningful goals. That wisdom emerges as four themes that underlie a model of coherent leadership. That is, the coherent leader will advisedly (a) know and nurture core values, (b) lead congruently, (c) compound capacity, and (d) expand consequence.

KNOW AND NURTURE CORE VALUES

Stephen Hawking (2001) succinctly described the origin and unfolding of the universe from the perspective of the big bang hypothesis: "The universe began in a big bang, a point where the whole universe, and everything in it, was scrunched up into a single point of infinite density. What results is an ever-expanding universe" (p. 79). Within that explanation, the point where the universe began is known as a singularity, the super dense compaction of all the matter in the universe. It is from that infinitesimal concentration of elemental building blocks that the resulting big bang created a universe that keeps expanding outward.

An analogy can be drawn here to the center from which leadership emanates. The exercise and potential of leadership is fueled and oriented by a solid foundation of core values. As Patrick Sayne described it, orientation to such a density of conviction leaves a leader little choice about the direction to be followed or the action to be taken: "You have to be able to quit your job for what you believe in." Kuami Pianim took that perspective further in suggesting that, if what you believe is truly a core value, you have to be ready to die for it.

In Chapters 1 through 3, the profiled leaders described leadership formation as a process that evolved across four integrated stages.

1. Leaders build and test their values through interactions with their environment and significant others.

2. Leaders further define and articulate their values through exploration of vocational callings and by making the most of challenges, experimenting with work, and finding opportunities to spread their wings.

3. Leaders commit to their values and callings by building competence and seeing the results of their efforts.

4. Leaders are compelled to accept the mantle of leadership, often through necessity, to fulfill their values and commitments.

Notably, the values that developed during the leaders' formation experiences continued to be refined after they had assumed leadership roles. Being a leader provided ample opportunity to test and solidify core values and commitments.

Figure 10.1 lists the values most commonly described and advocated by the 36 leaders. Such values were forged during leadership formation as each leader's worldview was shaped by context and then refined by calling, commitment, and the assumption of a leadership role. At the same time that values were being tested and applied in early life experiences, that very experience further shaped and reinforced core values. Subsequently, the same reciprocal dynamic is observed throughout leadership performance and sustainability. Ultimately, a value dynamic is moving in both directions along a two-way trail, with terminal points in core values on one end and expanded leadership consequence on the other (again, see Figure 10.1).

So why might a leader attend to values? The 36 interviewed leaders made a case for core values as the wellspring that both motivates and aligns leadership performance and sustainability. Their observations additionally suggest that the exercise of value-aligned elements of leadership performance and sustainability continually validate and reenergize commitments to compelling

A. Values are constructed from contextual experience. For example, value for

   1. Human dignity, equality, and diversity

   2. Hard work and perseverance

   3. High standards of responsibility in self and others

   4. Competence, skill, and knowledge

   5. Productive thinking habits (e.g., analytic, creative)

   6. Service to others

   7. Making a difference in the world

B. Values become both an energy force and a product within coherent leadership. A coherent relationship between leadership formation, performance and sustainability arises from core values. Core values, in turn, are continually reinforced by elements of leadership performance and sustainability.

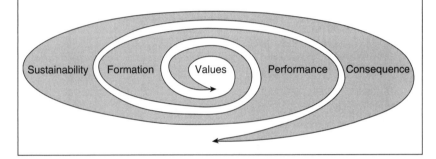

Figure 10.1   The Value Dynamic Within Leadership Coherence

purpose. Being aware of and regularly reflecting about one's values and their relationship to one's conduct appears to be well advised. Such reflection cuts to the literal center of leadership. Whatever the challenge, status, or context, the referencing of core values is useful when assessing the need for and conduct of leadership, particularly when the going gets tough. This orientation is also compatible with the conceptualization of transformational leadership—leadership that is purpose driven, inducing both leaders and followers to transcend personal interests in favor of the greater good (Burns, 1978; Bryman, 1992).

In effect, core values represent the fundamental element of a coherent leadership universe. They form the primal thread of an inner leadership coherence about purpose and commitment which, when established, invites a natural and logical weaving-in of leadership performance and sustainability. Further, as the core of values is wound progressively tighter, the foundation that supports and energizes leadership becomes increasingly solid and more powerful.

LEAD CONGRUENTLY

Wheatley and Kellner-Rogers (1996) noted that living systems are self-organizing and that organizations act in much the same way. From that perspective, they postulated that leaders must act from "intention, not a set of plans" (p. 7). Centered by their core values, the 36 interviewed leaders enjoyed clarity about their intentions. Inner coherence about commitment and purpose, in turn, led them to perform their leadership roles in a naturally congruent manner. That harmony between values and performance was most notably expressed in the form of character traits and behaviors aligned to the social, emotional, and cognitive nature of human capacity (see Figure 10.2).

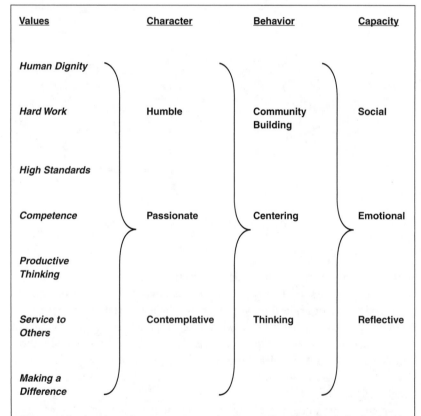

Values	Character	Behavior	Capacity
Human Dignity			
Hard Work	Humble	Community Building	Social
High Standards			
Competence	Passionate	Centering	Emotional
Productive Thinking			
Service to Others	Contemplative	Thinking	Reflective
Making a Difference			

Congruent leadership performance emerges from core values that shape the leadership character and behavior that in turn influence the capacity of others toward the achievement of goals. Such alignment represents a natural and logical (i.e., coherent) relationship etween what leaders value, who they are, and what they do that productively connects them to organizational capacity.

Figure 10.2   An Example of Leadership Performance Congruence

Harmony between leadership practice and core values and commitments holds advantage in its potential for realizing unity and integration of effect. The opposite circumstance would be necessarily true for leaders who are "out of alignment" with a belief system, resulting in incongruent leadership performance and fragmented outcomes. Goleman, Boyatzis, and McKee (2002) have suggested that when such lack of congruence exists, a dissonance occurs that is detrimental to the emotional health of an organization.

The other important element within this assessment of leadership congruency is that harmony between values and performance, while valuable and desirable in itself, must also extend to a harmonious relationship with the very nature of human capacity. That is, given leaders who are clear about their values and purpose and who have congruent character and behavior, it remains that their character and behavior must effectively connect to how human systems best learn and achieve. In effect then, leaders must get three things right and in congruent alignment. They must be clear about values and commitments, congruent in character and behavior in general, and congruent in character and behavior that effectively engages the nature of human capacity.

As it happened, the interviewed leaders described congruency within their leadership experience that was marked by character traits and behaviors that were prominently aligned to social, emotional, and reflective dimensions of human capacity for growth and achievement. It must be emphasized, however, that the particular values, traits, and behaviors advocated by the 36 leaders, regardless of how attractive and universal they might appear to be, are not the only values, traits, and behaviors to be adopted and exercised by leaders. It is also important to acknowledge that leaders undoubtedly connect to human capacity in dimensions and ways beyond those described in the conversations we have examined in this conversation. The point that can be made is that there was such congruency and alignment across the leadership experience of this diverse group of exemplary leaders. Is such congruency important? One might best answer that question by reflecting on the prospects for success of the 36 leaders had they not established such congruency between what they valued, their character and behavior, and how they connected to those they aspired to influence.

COMPOUND CAPACITY

Beyond nurturing core values and leading congruently, the reflections of 36 leaders suggest that there is wisdom in adopting dispositions and strategies that compound capacity and sustain leadership over time.

Collins (2001) observed that great companies are headed by great leaders who are able to take their organizations to a new state of being. They do so, in part, by consistently encouraging solution seeking, innovation, continuous learning, and systemic thinking aligned to organizational mission. Such perception of what makes the leadership difference was also evident within the stories of the interviewed leaders. They described themselves as being particularly disposed toward being

1. Centered on compelling purpose

2. Analytic in assessing problems and options

3. Creative in generating alternatives and opportunities

4. Positive in outlook

5. Persistent in pursuit of goals

6. Curious about new information and possibilities

7. Invested in developing the capacity of others

Such dispositions represented what the leaders perceived to be the essence of their leadership character and behavior. More important, it was how they established an enduring effect on the culture of their organization. Dispositions in thinking and behavior were the means by which the leaders moved beyond leadership of the moment to sustainable leadership. They aspired to promote organizational cultures that were focused on purpose and disposed toward analytic and creative thinking, collaboration, positive persistence in effort, and the pursuit of new knowledge and challenge. It was through the cultivation and exercise of productive dispositions of thinking and behavior, both in themselves and in others, that the leaders elevated the sustainability to their leadership influence on the achievement of goals. Such cultivation of capacity is consistent with Bennis's (2004) observation that gifted leaders see their primary responsibility as that of unleashing the talents of others so that a collective vision might be realized.

The interviewed leaders also adopted strategies for maintaining their personal viability and endurance within leadership roles that were physically, mentally, and emotionally demanding—strategies that sustained the leader behind the leadership. Specifically, they consciously aspired to

1. Stay physically fit

2. Manage emotions to their mental and physical advantage

3. Value counsel from family, friends, and colleagues

4. Create space for maintaining clarity and perspective

5. Get charged by the challenges and results associated with their commitments

6. Seek intellectual stimulation

7. Welcome inspiration from connection to higher purpose

The valuable advice about compounding capacity, then, is that sustaining dispositions and strategies collectively elevate leadership to enduring influence and legacy. Congruent leadership will get a leader into the game, but the compounding of capacity in self and others is a product of leadership sustainability. It is a matter of staying in the game and developing enduring influence through productive habits that ultimately make the leadership difference.

EXPAND CONSEQUENCE

Mihaly Csikzentmihalyi (1991) describes happiness as the state of flow, a state where our ability is matched with our interest to such an extent that we are operating in kairos (natural) rather than chronos (precise) time. We become totally immersed in whatever we are doing in a flow state such that time seems to stand still. You look up from an engaging book and find that it is 2 A.M., you are working on an intriguing problem and hours disappear, or you are conversing with a dear friend and miss an appointment.

The concept of flow is useful to understanding the idea of coherent leadership. For the coherent leader, a flow emerges from an inner coherence about values and purpose; it moves on through aligned character and behavior to bond with capacity and then to the compounding of capacity through sustaining dispositions and strategies. It is the culminating effect of this flow—a natural and logical relationship between leadership purpose, performance, and sustainability—that leadership consequence is enhanced by a coherence that is both efficient and cyclical (see Figure 10.3).

Leadership formation, as previously noted, provides the foundation from which the alignment of leadership coherence flows. Such alignment, moreover, appears to be iterative in nature. The interviewed leaders described how they developed greater certainty about their purpose, performance, and sustaining dispositions and strategies by revisiting their value base often in light of experience. Consequently, core values were strengthened and grew more powerful in their influence on leadership practice.

Hawking (2001), again, notes that from the density of a singularity comes the energy to not only create a universe, but to also maintain an ever-expanding ripple. Thus would appear to be the case with coherent leadership. A dense core of values and commitments forged in leadership formation brings forth coherence about compelling purpose and then continues to ripple through leadership performance and sustainability with the ultimate effect of ever-expanding leadership consequence.

The advice within this part of the story, then, is that a leader seeking coherence of leadership purpose, performance, and sustainability will consciously reflect on how values are flowing through his or her leadership universe—and to what consequence of effect. To that end, a leader might be well served by a model of coherent leadership.

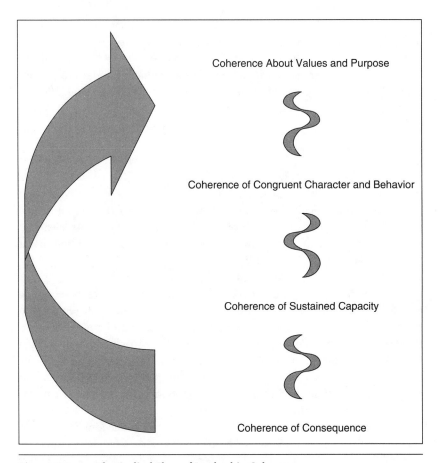

Coherence About Values and Purpose

Coherence of Congruent Character and Behavior

Coherence of Sustained Capacity

Coherence of Consequence

Figure 10.3   The Cyclical Flow of Leadership Coherence

A Model of Coherent Leadership

The cliché about the whole being greater than the sum of its parts applies to the model for leadership coherence that emerged from this research. The questions put to 36 leaders inquired about leadership formation, performance, and sustainability. The interviewed leaders provided rich descriptive responses to those questions, and many specific and helpful insights were thus revealed. But the unexpected revelation also occurred, and that was, and is, a good thing.

When planning a trip, a destination and route are determined to ensure a safe and timely arrival. The last time you planned a vacation, for example, you likely selected a desirable location; mapped the air, land, or water routes to get there; and secured related accommodations. Depending on how well organized you like to be, you might have also prepared daily itineraries of activities and events. However well planned, nevertheless, a vacation almost always encounters the unexpected. The good side of such unanticipated events is that they often generate memorable moments of discovery and inspiration—dramatic encounters with weather and topography, detours that connect to history and geography heretofore unknown, or chance acquaintances with interesting people.

The point is that, although planning and anticipation in any human endeavor is almost always necessary and recommended, it is from the unfolding of unanticipated developments that the most rewarding experiences and insights are realized. This pattern of benefit from the unexpected, moreover, is strongly embraced by qualitative research.

Within any research effort, planning is required, but by its defining alignment to the inductive process, qualitative research must remain open to possibilities. Thus, this inquiry was guided by a plan to interview an eclectic group of exemplary leaders from diverse contexts around the world about leadership formation, performance, and sustainability. The leaders were interviewed according to a set protocol (see Figure 2 in the Introduction) to prompt a collective reflection and, thereby, discover salient patterns about how they came to leadership, performed as leaders, and sustained their leadership influence over time and challenge. Given this research approach, the expected happened. That is, the leaders did reveal prominent patterns of experience, value orientation, character, behavior, disposition, and strategy. The unanticipated insight also emerged, however, as the leaders' reflections progressively told a story that described a larger pattern of leadership coherence. It was a pattern, as has been described in preceding sections of this chapter, that could be observed as moving from the internalization of core goals and commitments during formative life experience toward a congruency with leadership performance and sustainability and back again. It was not only a pattern of natural and logical connections that moved from formation to performance to sustainability. It was also a pattern that observed a reciprocal relationship in that what the leaders did to sustain their leadership reinforced their performance, and performance, in turn, reinforced core values nested at the heart of the leaders' formative experience (see Figure 10.4).

In other words, it became evident that the process of leadership formation was inextricably linked to how the leaders performed and maintained their ability to do so over time. It also appeared that within this tight pattern of coherence from formation through sustainability lies a key as to how leaders realize an expanded consequence of their leadership influence and achievement.

Ultimately, as the patterns were discovered and the puzzle pieces assembled, it was coherence—a natural, logical, and consistent relationship of parts—that defined the leaders' collective leadership story. It was a story about the phenomenon of leadership coherence in which leaders aligned value formation with congruent performance and compounding sustainability to achieve

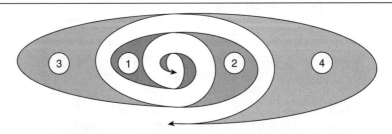

1. Leadership *formation* forges an inner coherence of core values, vocational calling and commitment to lead.
2. An inner coherence about values, callings, and commitments is subsequently extended through congruent leadership *performance* aligned to the nature of human capacity.
3. A coherency between elements of leadership formation and performance is further extended to leadership *sustainability* through dispositions and strategies that elevate leadership influence.
4. A dynamic coherency between the elements of leadership formation, performance, and sustainability expands leadership *consequence*.

Figure 10.4   A Model of Coherent Leadership

compelling purpose. Formation oriented their leadership influence, performance executed their leadership influence, and sustainability maintained and compounded their leadership influence. The more coherent the relationship between those three elements was, the greater was the expansion of the consequence of their leadership legacy. The reflections of the interviewed leaders also suggest that leadership coherence is a dynamic process that continues to evolve over a lifetime of leadership practice.

With that, we leave you with a model that will hopefully be of service to your interest in bringing further coherence to your leadership practice. We also leave your reflection about this chapter content to the Extended Conversation exercises that follow in Chapter 11.

11

An Ongoing Conversation

Organizations and communities are made of conversations.

—Perkins (2003, p. 123)

The Class Act

The reflections shared by the interviewed leaders about their formation, performance, and sustainability provide examples from which other leaders might learn and further reflect. Their collective story also helps us conceptualize a model of leadership coherence. That model builds on the definition of leadership as a process of influencing others toward the achievement of goals. Specifically, it proposes that leadership that is coherently connected in values, performance, and sustainability holds promise for an expanded consequence of influence on the achievement of goals. The stories that unfolded from 36 exemplary leaders spoke to the effect of such coherence in their leadership experience. It is a perspective of leadership coherence that is very reinforcing of the old adage, "Get your act together." From such perspective, the leadership stories shared by the interviewed leaders established their status as coherent leaders. They had their leadership acts coherently together. They were, as it were, class acts.

What, then, about your leadership act? In thinking back about why you chose to read this book, it can be assumed that you had a general interest in understanding more about leadership. Perhaps your motivation was simply to explore additional insights about leadership or to pick up some specific tips about leadership preparation or how effective leaders perform their roles. Now that you have read the preceding 10 chapters, we hope you have found the stories shared by 36 leaders from around the world to be of value to your initial reading interests. We also hope that you have been an active contributor, as the 37th storyteller, to the leadership conversations conducted across Chapters 1 through 9. Most of all, we want to encourage your further reflection about the coherence of your leadership act.

While it is always enlightening to access the wisdom of other leaders, the leadership story is an ongoing tale and, ultimately, a personal account. This particular opportunity for leadership conversation has visited with leaders from five continents. As with most travels, however, the road eventually leads back home. So it is that this last chapter is yours for reflection about where your leadership coherence is, where it might go from here, and how you will keep it going.

The Current State

To assess the current state of your leadership coherence, you are invited to engage the sequence of advice offered in Chapter 10 about nurturing core values, leading coherently, compounding capacity, and expanding consequence (see Figure 11.1). Your assessment will be facilitated by Exercises 11.1–11.4.

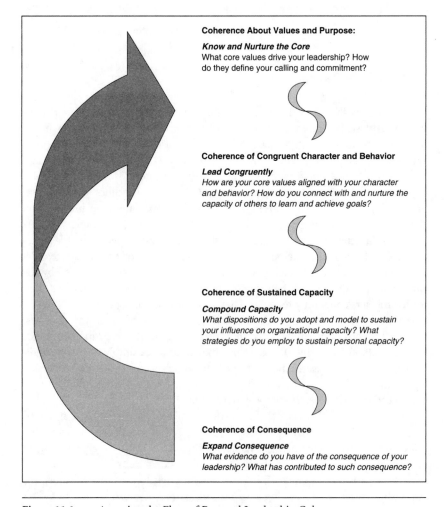

Coherence About Values and Purpose:

Know and Nurture the Core
What core values drive your leadership? How do they define your calling and commitment?

Coherence of Congruent Character and Behavior

Lead Congruently
How are your core values aligned with your character and behavior? How do you connect with and nurture the capacity of others to learn and achieve goals?

Coherence of Sustained Capacity

Compound Capacity
What dispositions do you adopt and model to sustain your influence on organizational capacity? What strategies do you employ to sustain personal capacity?

Coherence of Consequence

Expand Consequence
What evidence do you have of the consequence of your leadership? What has contributed to such consequence?

Figure 11.1   Assessing the Flow of Personal Leadership Coherence

---

EXERCISE 11.1   Further Conversation: Know and Nurture Core Values

A. What core values drive your leadership?

B. How do they define your calling and commitment to lead?

EXERCISE 11.2   Further Conversation: Lead Congruently

A. How are your core values aligned with your leadership character and behavior?

B. How does your leadership character and behavior help you connect to others and facilitate their capacity to contribute to the achievement of goals?

EXERCISE 11.3   Further Conversation: Compound Capacity

A. What dispositions do you adopt and model to sustain your influence on organizational capacity?

B. What strategies do you employ to sustain personal capacity?

EXERCISE 11.4   Further Conversation: Expand Consequences

A. What evidence do you have of the consequences of your leadership?

B. What has contributed to such consequences?

The Preferred State

Each of the interviewed leaders traveled a life journey toward consequential leadership, intuitively nurturing a coherency between their values, how they performed their responsibilities, and how they sustained their influence. Having assessed the current coherency status of your leadership journey, you should have a sharpened awareness of what aspects of your leadership universe are in alignment and what needs attention.

Exercise 11.5 will facilitate your reflection about what is most important to attend to if you are to realize greater coherency and effect in your leadership future. To that end, this reflection asks that you examine the barriers that might inhibit or detract from the coherency of your leadership experience, as well as important supportive elements that might enhance coherent leadership. You will see that this exercise is a modified force-field analysis designed to focus your next steps toward aligned leadership practice.

The Continuing Conversation

Our conversation with 37 leaders (i.e., conversation with the 36 interviewed leaders and you) ends here. It is a conversation that is to be continued, however, by leaders who cultivate an appreciation for wholeness and unity in their leadership experience.

So we leave you now with a final Further Conversation reflection task. That is to decide how you might best advance your conversation about leadership formation, performance, and sustainability from this point.

Whatever the contributions of the conversation facilitated by this book, it goes without saying that there are many other worthy conversations that are and will be available to you. It comes down to how proactive you will be in seeking out and participating in such exchanges of experience and insight.

You can expect to continue to grow and evolve in the coherency of your leadership from such ongoing conversation.

EXERCISE 11.5 Further Conversation: Force Field Analysis of Leadership Coherence		
Forces That Restrict	Elements of Coherence	Forces That Support
_____	Clear Values	_____
_____		_____
_____		_____
_____		_____
_____	Commitment	_____
_____		_____
_____		_____
_____	Value-Aligned Character	_____
_____		_____
_____		_____
_____	Value-Aligned Behavior	_____
_____		_____
_____		_____
_____	Connections to Capacity	_____
_____		_____
_____	• Social	_____
_____	• Emotional	_____
_____	• Reflective	_____
_____	• Other	_____
_____		_____
_____	Dispositions That Sustain Organizational Capacity	_____
_____		_____
_____		_____
_____	Strategies That Sustain Personal Capacity	_____
_____		_____
_____		_____

The most supportive force(s): _____

The most restrictive force(s): _____

Actions that will advance support and resolve restrictions: _____

_____

_____

EXERCISE 11.6   Further Conversation

A. What leadership-related book(s) will you read next?

B. What professional conferences will you participate in in the near future?

C. How, when, and where will you arrange to have conversations about leadership

With colleagues?

With others?

D. How will you arrange for space and time for individual reflection about your leadership experience?

Your core values?

Your character and behavior?

Your influence on the capacity of others?

The dispositions you employ to sustain organizational capacity?

Strategies you employ to sustain personal capacity?

Forces that restrict or support your leadership?

Epilogue

The Continuing Quest

The good to great executives were all cut from the same cloth. It didn't matter whether their company was consumer or industrial, in crisis or steady state, offered services or products. . . . All the good to great companies had Level 5 leadership . . . which cuts against the grain of conventional wisdom. . . . [They] are a study in duality: modest and willful, humble and fearless.

—Collins (2001, p. 22).

In his book *Good to Great* (2001), Collins described Level 5 leaders, who embodied a compelling vision, modeled commitment and humility, and empowered others toward success while keeping an eye on results. It is noteworthy that, while Collins was generally looking for what promoted exceptional organizational success, his research drew him to this unique type of leader as a key factor behind the transition of an organization from good to great. It is also worth noting that the leaders that populated this study described similar attributes.

One by one, 36 leaders shared their stories and reflected on things familiar but perhaps not previously articulated. Not surprising, the power of sharing their experience progressively led to greater introspection during the interview process, leading to comments such as "I never said this before" and "I had not thought of it this way previously, but now I see it." Such is the power of "talking story," allowing wisdom to be both constructed and disclosed by simply asking a question and taking the time to listen.

It is our hope that you will take time to ask questions of yourself and others as you continue on your leadership journey and to listen to both your inner voice and the voice of others. Whether you generate insight similar to that revealed in *Leading Coherently* is not an issue. What is important is the examination of the relationship between your internal motivation to lead and your outer expressions of aligned practice. Perhaps the most important lesson here is that a commitment to lead and lead well requires a parallel commitment to pursue leadership coherence—to continually reflect on who you are, where you are going, and how you are conducting yourself as a leader. As Ulice Payne put it, "I am who I am. It's me. It's what I do. You have to believe it and live the commitment. If you don't have it, it won't last. . . . It has to come from within."

It is difficult to adequately express our gratitude to the 36 leaders who were willing to invest their time and insights in this project. Their generosity, candor, and ability to express their leadership journeys so eloquently led to this story about coherent leadership. They were willing to open their life experiences to us, and they were agreeable to our charge of sharing it with you. We hope that their stories fuel your commitment to becoming a more coherent leader and that you realize great consequence from such effort.

References

Alvesson, M. (1996). Leadership studies: From procedure and abstraction to reflexivity and situation. *Leadership Quarterly, 7*, 455–485.

American Heritage Dictionary (4th ed.). (2000). Boston: Houghton Mifflin.

Antonakis, J., Cianciolo, A. T., & Sternberg, R. J. (2004). *The nature of leadership.* Thousand Oaks, CA: Sage.

Ayman, R. (2004). Situational and contingency approaches to leadership. In J. Antonakis, A. T. Cianciolo, & R. J. Sternberg (Eds.), *The nature of leadership* (pp. 148–170). Thousand Oaks, CA: Sage.

Bandura, A. (1997). *Self-efficacy: The exercise of control.* New York: Freeman.

Barth, R. S. (2003). *Lessons learned: Shaping relationships and the culture of the workplace.* Thousand Oaks, CA: Corwin.

Bass, B. M. (1997). Does the transactional–transformational leadership paradigm transcend organizational and national boundaries? *American Psychologist, 52*, 130–139.

Bass, B. M. (1998). *Transformational leadership: Industrial, military, and educational impact.* Mahwah, NJ: Erlbaum.

Bennis, W. (2004). The crucibles of authentic leadership. In J. Antonakis, A. T. Cianciolo, & R. J. Sternberg (Eds.), *The nature of leadership* (pp. 331–342). Thousand Oaks, CA: Sage.

Bossidy, L., & Charan, R. (2002). *Execution: The discipline of getting things done.* New York: Crown Press.

Bryman, A. (1992). Charisma and leadership in organizations. London: Sage.

Burns, J. M. (1978). *Leadership.* New York: Harper & Row.

Center for Leadership Studies. (2000). *Multifactor leadership questionnaire: Norms.* Retrieved June 1, 2004, from http://cls.binghamton.edu/mlq.htm

Collins, J. (2001). *Good to great.* New York: HarperCollins.

Connett, M., & Carmera, J. (2001). Who will lead? *Stanford Business Review, 69*(3), 12–13.

Costa, A. L., & Kallick, B. (Eds.). (2000). *Discovering and exploring habits of mind.* Alexandria, VA: Association for Supervision and Curriculum Development.

Covey, S. R. (1989). *The seven habits of highly effective people: Restoring the character ethic.* New York: Simon & Schuster.

Csikszentmihalyi, M. (1991). *Flow: The psychology of optimal experience.* New York: Perennial.

Daft, R. L., & Lengel, R. H. (1998). *Fusion leadership: Unlocking the subtle forces that change people and organizations.* San Francisco: Berrett-Koehler.

Daloz, L. P., Keen, C. H., Keen J. P., & Parks, S. D. (1997). *Common fire: Leading lives of commitment in a complex world*. Boston: Beacon Press.

Day, D. V. (2000). Leadership development: A review in context. *Leadership Quarterly, 11,* 581–613.

Day, D. V. (2001). Assessment of leadership outcomes. In S. J. Zaccaro & R. J. Klimoski (Eds.), *The nature of organizational leadership* (pp. 384–409). San Francisco: Jossey-Bass.

Den Hartog, D. N., House, R. J., Hanges, P. J., Ruiz-Quintanilla, S. A., Dorfman, P. W., Koopman, P. L., et al. (1999). Culture specific and cross-culturally generalizable implicit leadership theories: Are attributes of charismatic/transformational leadership universally endorsed? *The Leadership Quarterly, 10,* 219–256.

Denison, D. R. (1997). *Corporate culture and organizational effectiveness*. Ann Arbor, MI: Author.

Dewey, J. (1933). *How we think: A restatement of the relation of reflective thinking to the educative process*. Boston: Houghton Mifflin.

Dickmann, M. H., and Stanford-Blair, N. (2002). *Connecting leadership to the brain*. Thousand Oaks, CA: Corwin.

Dickmann, M. H., Stanford-Blair, N., & Rosati-Bojar, A. (2004). *Leading with the brain in mind: 101 brain-compatible practices for leaders*. Thousand Oaks, CA: Corwin.

Emerson, R. W. (1911). *The conduct of life, nature and other essays*. London: Dent.

Ferrandino, V., & Tirozzi, G. (2000, October 18). The shortage of principals continues. *Education Week, 20,* 7, p. 18.

Fullan, M. (2001). *Leading in a culture of change*. San Francisco: Jossey-Bass.

Fullan, M. (2003). *The moral imperative of school leadership*. Thousand Oaks, CA: Corwin.

Gardner, H. (1995). *Leading minds: An anatomy of leadership*. New York: Basic Books.

Gardner, J. W. (1990). On leadership. New York: Free Press.

Gilman, R. (1990). Sustainability. The state of movement. *In Context, 25,* pp. 10–14.

Gladwell, M. (2000). *The tipping point: How little things can make a big difference*. New York: Little, Brown.

Goleman, D., Boyatzis, R. E., & McKee, A. (2002). *Primal leadership: Realizing the power of emotional intelligence*. Cambridge, MA: Harvard Business School Press.

Greenleaf, R. K. (1996). *On becoming a servant leader*. San Francisco: Jossey-Bass.

Hawking, S. (2001). *The universe in a nutshell*. New York: Bantam.

Johnson, R. T., & Johnson, D. W. (1991). Cooperative learning. Minneapolis, MN: Burgess Press.

Kauffman, S. (1995). *At home in the universe: The search for chaos, self-organization and complexity*. Oxford, UK: Oxford University Press.

Kiersey, D., & Bates, M. (1984). *Please understand me*. Prometheus.

Kouzes, J. M., & Posner, B. Z. (1995). *The leadership challenge: How to get extraordinary things done in organizations*. San Francisco: Jossey-Bass.

Leider, R. J. (1997). *The power of purpose: Creating meaning in your life and work*. San Francisco: Berrett-Koehler.

Lowe, K. B., & Gardner, W. L. (2000). Ten years of *The Leadership Quarterly*: Contributions and challenges for the future. *Leadership Quarterly, 11,* 459–514.

Lowe, K. B., Kroeck, K. G., & Sivasubramaniam, N. (1996). Effectiveness correlates of transformational and transaction leadership: A meta-analytic review of the MLQ literature. *Leadership Quarterly, 7,* 385–425.

Mandela, N. (1995). *Long walk to freedom.* New York: Back Bay Books.

Marzano, R., & Pickering, D. (1997). *Dimensions of learning.* Alexandria, VA: Association of Supervision and Curriculum Development.

McCauley, C. D. (2001). Leader training and development. In S. J. Zaccaro & R. J. Klimoske (Eds.), *The nature of organizational leadership* (pp. 347–383). San Francisco: Jossey-Bass.

McCauley, C. D., Moxley, R. S., & Van Velsor, E. (Eds.). (1998). *The Center for Creative Leadership handbook for leadership development.* San Francisco: Jossey-Bass.

McKay, H. (1996). *Swim with the sharks without being eaten alive.* New York: Ballantine.

Miscisin, M., & Haines, J. (2001). *Showing our true colors.* Riverside, CA: True Colors.

Morton-Cooper, A., & Palmer, A. (2000). *Mentoring, preceptorship and clinical supervision* (2nd ed.). UK: Blackwell Science.

Ornstein, R. (1997). *The right mind: Making sense of the hemispheres.* New York: Harcourt Brace.

Patton, M. Q. (1991). *Qualitative research and evaluation methods.* Thousand Oaks, CA: Sage.

Perkins, D. (1995). *Outsmarting IQ: The emerging science of learnable intelligence.* New York: Free Press.

Perkins, D. (2003). *King Arthur's round table: How collaborative conversations create smart organizations.* Hoboken, NJ: Wiley.

Ridley, M. (2003). *Nature via nurture: Genes, experience and what makes us human.* New York: Perennial.

Rost, J. C. (1993). *Leadership for the twenty-first century.* Westport, CT: Praeger.

Sashkin, M. (2003). *Leadership that matters.* San Francisco: Berrett-Koehler.

Sashkin, M. (2004). Transformational leadership approaches: A review and synthesis. In J. Antonakis, A. T. Cianciolo, & R. J. Sternberg (Eds.), *The nature of leadership* (pp. 331–342). Thousand Oaks, CA: Sage.

Senge, P. M. (1990). *The fifth discipline: The art and practice of the learning organization.* New York: Doubleday.

Siedman, I. (1998). *Interviewing as qualitative research: A guide for researchers in education and the social science.* New York: Teachers College Press.

Watts, D. J. (2003). *Six degrees: The science of a connected age.* New York: Norton.

Wheatley, M. J. (1992). *Leadership and the new science: Learning about organization from an orderly universe.* San Francisco: Berrett-Koehler.

Wheatley, M. J. (2002). *Turning to one another: Simple conversations to restore hope to the future.* San Francisco: Berrett-Koehler.

Wheatley, M. J., & Kellner-Rogers, M. (1996). *A simpler way.* San Francisco: Berrett-Koehler.

Zaccaro, S. J., Kemp, C., & Bader, P. (2004). Leadership traits and attributes. In J. Antonakis, A. T. Cianciolo, & R. J. Sternberg (Eds.), *The nature of leadership* (pp. 101–124). Thousand Oaks, CA: Sage.

Zipkin, A. (2000, May 31). The wisdom of thoughtfulness. *New York Times,* pp. C1, C10.

Index

About the Authors

Nancy Stanford-Blair and Michael H. Dickmann are Professors of Leadership Studies at Cardinal Stritch University in Milwaukee, Wisconsin. They also are Associates of the Leadership Center at Cardinal Stritch University. In their university roles, the authors teach, advise, and conduct research in the areas of leadership, learning, and service. They also serve as consultants to education, business, and service organizations in matters of leadership, learning, and organizational development.